GW01034025

"Give Asthma the Big <u>A</u>*"*

How One Australian Woman Beat Asthma!

Marian Shepherd Slee

Published by Bookman Press
325 Flinders Lane
Melbourne Vic 3000
Australia

ISBN 1 86359 152 0

Copyright © 1996 Marian Shepherd Slee

PUBLISHER'S NOTE
The information contained is this book is not intended as a
substitute for consulting your physician. All matters regarding
your health require medical supervision.

All rights reserved. No part of this publication may be
reproduced, stored in a retrieval system, or transmitted in any
form or by any means electronic, mechanical, photocopying,
recording or otherwise without the prior permission of the
publisher.

Every effort has been made to ensure that this book is free from
error or omissions. However, the Publisher, the Editor, or their
respective employees or agents, shall not accept responsibility
for injury, loss or damage occasioned to any person acting or
refraining from action as a result of material in this book
whether or not such injury, loss, damage is in any way due to
any negligent act or omission, breach of duty or default on the
part of the Publisher, the Editor, or their respective employees or
agents.

National Library of Australia
Cataloguing-in-Publication entry

Shepherd-Slee, Marian,
Give Asthma The Big A

Includes index
1. Allergy - Australia - Popular works. 2. Asthma - Popular
works. 3. Vitamin A - Popular works. I. Title.

ISBN 1 86395 152 0

Printed by Griffin Paperbacks, Adelaide SA.
Cover Photo by Anthony Stolting

ABOUT THE AUTHOR

Marian grew up in the Central Queensland town of Biloela. She and husband, Jim, now reside in Brisbane, and have six adult children.

At age 27, Marian developed asthma and suffered regularly for eight years. In 1980, she accidentally stumbled across the amazing effects of vitamins A and E on her asthma. After three years of successfully treating herself, she felt compelled to spread the message to others. Letters to the Editor, Talk Back Radio and magazine articles were some of her methods.

She attempted to influence health professionals, and although some surprised her by their acceptance, the majority were negative. The feedback from followers of this treatment, however, has always been positive, and is typified by this response from the mother of an asthmatic child:

> *'If they invented a drug as good as this, it would be hailed a wonder drug.'*

ACKNOWLEDGEMENTS

I wish to express my sincere thanks to the following people: Betty, for her invaluable editing skills and endless patience; Beverley, for her encouragement throughout the years; Helen, Kerrie, Cameron and Luke for their generous assistance; and all who contributed their personal case histories.

Finally, to the members of my family, my appreciation and love for their continual support.

DEDICATION

This book is dedicated to all whose lives have been affected by asthma.

CONTENTS

FOREWORD

In Australia, asthma causes considerable mortality.

Perhaps due to changing environment and lifestyle; and despite modern medical intervention; the number of deaths from asthma has increased quite dramatically in the last decade.

Marian has uncovered a remarkable treatment approach, and I have found it of considerable help to my asthmatic patients time and time again.

Vitamin A acts by maintaining the integrity of epithelial cells. It protects the lining of the respiratory tract and acts as a barrier to chest infection. It is a simple and remarkably effective remedy.

Lyndal Hunter
Naturopath and Social Worker

INTRODUCTION

The alarming increase in asthma deaths is the catalyst for this book. In it I describe my discovery of a unique, simple but controversial management and prevention program for this disease.

News of untimely asthma deaths motivated me to share what I've learnt from fourteen years of research and experimentation. Watching fellow sufferers enduring the side-effects of drugs because no alternative treatment is countenanced, distressed me.

Now, in the nineties, the buzz words: 'What works is peer to peer' emphasises the growing recognition that those in the same situation can be of immense help to each other.

Do only medical authorities write about asthma? Most would agree that experts, though highly knowledgeable, do not feel the symptoms of this disease, or the effects of orthodox treatment — unless they themselves are asthmatic.

Each time an authority extols the virtues of drug therapy while dismissing the possibility of effective alternatives, I see <u>red</u>.

I am confident the message contained within this book will be good news for asthmatics everywhere. This treatment, when fully accepted, has never in my experience, been known to fail.

BECOMING AN ASTHMATIC

Asthma — I had it, now I don't.

In the past, I dreaded every respiratory infection and change in the season, now I live as though asthma was never a part of my life.

Allow me to tell you the story of my affliction and subsequent liberation.

Asthma became a reality for me in the winter of 1969. I was twenty-seven, married and the mother of three small boys. Earlier that year we were transferred to Brisbane and in the August I contracted Hong Kong 'Flu.

Each time I attempted to stand, severe infection and high temperatures made me faint and fall. I was worried. How could I feed my three-month-old son if I couldn't even stand? With help, I managed two days in bed and felt quite well apart from a raw feeling in the chest, and a suspicion I wasn't breathing properly. This unfamiliar feeling was disturbing; but a couple of weeks later these symptoms disappeared. Nonetheless, my lungs were never the same again.

Prior to this illness, any cold or influenza would disappear in a week, but following this episode I was prone to chest infections which responded only to antibiotics. I was puzzled. Formerly, I had rarely been afflicted with so much as a cough, and now a type of chronic bronchitis had developed — I was continually coughing up foul sputum.

One night I intimated to a doctor that I thought something sinister was occurring. She dismissed my fears and proceeded to ask, 'How do you feel in yourself?' She obviously believed I was seeking attention and saw nothing unusual about my symptoms. Feeling like a raging hypochondriac, I crept out of the surgery. 'Maybe,' I thought, 'everyone in Brisbane suffers with chest problems and they simply ignore the whole thing.'

I should mention here that it pains me to even mildly criticise this doctor. In the sixties, women doctors were rare. Lady Phyllis Cilento was, in my opinion, an absolute genius, and on the occasions I've encountered other women doctors, their empathy and concern have been extremely soothing. Women, in particular, need women doctors.

To return to my story. After two years of frequent chest infections, I awoke about 3.00am to hear a high pitched whistle coming from my chest. At first I was intrigued, but after two hours the whistling was still sounding, and I realised there would be no more sleep. This nocturnal wheezing continued over the following nights, and the resulting exhaustion (produced by lack of sleep combined with the demands of motherhood) often reduced me to tears.

Following these episodes, I was diagnosed 'Asthmatic' and prescribed both salbutamol and antibiotics. Luckily the antibiotics alone were sufficient because I could never force myself to use the puffer. To my mind, once I used that thing I would be admitting I was an asthmatic. You must remember, during the sixties the general view of asthma was that it was a psychosomatic disease; my pride couldn't handle that. The puffer frightened me — it seemed so abnormal and I have always had an aversion to unnatural things. Perhaps others shared my opinion of the puffer, because most asthmatics at that time tended to use it furtively.

At thirty years of age, I fell pregnant again.

From the very first month of that pregnancy I was plagued with chest infections. By the fourth month I'd had three episodes and had completed three courses of antibiotics. A couple of weeks later I succumbed to yet another chest infection. Fears for the baby's health prompted me to forego all antibiotics. Although asthma did not develop, the cough resulting from this infection was unbelievable — it had a definite graveyard quality. My obstetrician said it was probably bronchiectasis but my general practitioner disagreed, stating it was merely bronchitis.

That dreadful cough continued through to the seventh month. My mother said 'You'll have it till the baby is born for sure. This pregnancy must be taking a lot out of you.' That cough was so embarrassing that I became a virtual recluse.

Then one day everything changed.

A saleswoman for Rawleigh's® products, came to my door. She had a range of natural vitamins in stock, and as my eldest son and I were prone to colds, I bought some natural vitamin C — and reeled at the price.

I decided to get my money's worth by asking her some questions about vitamins. She explained that natural vitamins are always more expensive than synthetic. I asked her 'Why is it, that although my son and I take vitamin C tablets regularly, we continually develop chest infections, while my husband who never bothers with vitamins at all, doesn't even catch a cold?'

'Your husband probably eats lots of foods containing vitamin A,' she said. 'Does he like cheese?'

'Does he like cheese? He's practically addicted to it.'

'Well, that could explain it.' She went on to tell me that before commencing with vitamin A herself, she had caught pneumonia twenty-one times and was prescribed antibiotics the size of a ten cent piece. Since she had been using vitamin A she hadn't developed pneumonia once.

Although I was inclined to divide everything she said by three, I was still very impressed by her knowledge of vitamins. Next day I bought some vitamin A from the chemist (much cheaper) and although I took only one capsule per day, the results were amazing. Within three days that cough had disappeared. Continuing with the vitamin until the end of the pregnancy, I suffered no more chest infections, and that horrid graveyard cough never returned.

EMOTIONAL ASPECTS

Bronchitis was now a thing of the past. Whenever I developed a cough I simply took vitamin A capsules for a couple of days. I found however, as time went on, I was becoming more and more afflicted with asthma. It was particularly troublesome at the change of the seasons when temperatures dropped suddenly.

Although my asthma attacks usually lasted no more than two days, they were stressful, in that they tended to cause chronic tiredness and emotional problems.

I think most asthmatics try to minimise the emotional trauma. When a person loses control of their life they become depressed.

They find themselves unable to function properly. Many fastidious housewives (I wish I was in this category) tell of the anguish of being unable to maintain their homes in what they feel is the necessary state of cleanliness.

For me, it was more a case of feeling inadequate and frustrated whenever I couldn't live up to the expectations of others. From that standpoint, I think asthma could be a definite cause of marital problems.

I was doing my best to cope with the children and the housework, when some friends from Rockhampton called in for a visit. It was lovely to see them and I managed to provide refreshments and make conversation, however, by the time they were ready to leave, I was in a haze of exhaustion.

Shortly after their departure, my husband rang. When I told him about the visit, he inquired,

'Did you ask them to stay for tea?'

'No, I didn't think of it.'

'You should have asked them to stay. They came all this way out and you didn't even ask them to stay?'

I was young, immature and terribly upset. I locked myself in the toilet and cried. As those who know me will verify, it takes considerable provocation to induce even a sniffle from me, but on that occasion I felt I'd been pushed over the edge.

I was five months pregnant and although I didn't know it, I was carrying twins. I did suspect that something was different because of the considerable pressure under the rib-cage. It felt as if my lungs were being squashed against my ribs. I had also been experiencing asthma symptoms for the previous two or three days, so I was completely miserable.

After crying myself out, I waddled into the kitchen and was absolutely stunned to see my husband standing there. It was only 3.00pm. 'What on earth are you doing here?' I asked.

'Well, you sounded pretty upset so I thought I'd better come home to check on you.'

I was completely dumbfounded. Jim wouldn't take time off work if Brisbane was hit by an earthquake.

I'm lucky to have such a concerned husband.

I really do feel for asthmatic males. Society expects men to be ever strong, reliable and, in Australia — sporty. Young boys and men who love to compete, and who base their manhood on their sporting prowess, must suffer dreadfully.

Asthmatic sporting heroes, such as Allan Border, Steve Mortimar, Neil Brooks, Steve Holland and others inspire much admiration. Of course, some of our top female athletes are also asthmatic: Dawn Fraser and Jenny Donnet spring to mind. What drive and will-power must they possess to overcome a handicap like asthma?

For twelve months following the birth of the twins, I was extremely healthy (which was just as well because sleep was such a rarity, I was on the verge of collapse). I don't know why I was asthma-free that year. I would never have coped if I had succumbed.

The following year, asthma returned in its previous form. During the winter and change of seasons, I would sleep with the windows in the bedroom closed and if it was cold, have the heater on all night. Keeping the bedroom warm seemed to improve my breathing. The worst hours were from 4.00am until dawn and the resulting lack of sleep often made life difficult.

How Jim tolerated the heat and stuffiness in the bedroom, I'll never know. Thank goodness he can sleep through anything.

One long weekend, the temperatures which had been fairly high up to that point, suddenly plummeted to a low of six degrees. This drop triggered asthma in both myself and our eldest son Danny, then aged eleven. At three years of age, this blonde, blue-eyed boy had been diagnosed with asthmatic bronchitis.

During that freezing holiday break, we two asthma sufferers locked ourselves in a bedroom, turned the heater up, and wheezed away all weekend. At the time we suffered more from 'troublesome' asthma than the 'frightening' variety. I can't even remember using medication apart from Elixophyllin® to help us through the night. We simply felt breathless, miserable, and were confined to bed (Incidentally Elixophyllin® always gave me a giant 'hangover' the next morning).

It wasn't until I was thirty-four that my first really frightening attack occurred.

FIRST SEVERE ATTACK

It was on a Good Friday, when we arrived home from a wonderful holiday at the beach. I remember sitting in church, my new sun-dress revealing a first-class tan, and thinking I had never felt fitter or healthier.

How quickly things change.

Between 3.00pm and 9.00pm the weather temperature dropped by about twelve degrees. We ate fish for tea as well, and although I didn't know it then, I'm now convinced I'm allergic to some seafood. By nine o'clock that evening, I was wondering if I would survive the night. This asthma attack was terrifying. The tightness in my chest was so severe that my lungs felt like blocks of cement and the effort to inhale and exhale was enormous. I should have found the puffer prescribed many years before, but I'd never used it, was still afraid of it, and imagined after all those years it would probably be ineffective.

Being an ex-lifesaver, Jim helped considerably by placing his hands on my rib-cage and pumping my lungs as one would a pair of bellows. He couldn't sustain this effort for long. My chest was feeling cold. I gasped, 'Could you fill the hot water bottle for me to cuddle?' Strangely the heat of that bottle seemed to be what was needed, because my breathing improved and I fell asleep. (I am not recommending placing hot water bottles on chests as a suitable treatment for asthma.)

Awakening the next morning, I felt so dreadful that I burst into tears. My mother, holidaying with us at the time, appeared shocked to see me so uncharacteristically emotional. In spite of her habitual distrust of doctors, she insisted I visit one immediately.

The doctor prescribed Quibron® tablets; however I received the distinct impression he was not interested in having me as a patient, although he had seemed to welcome our son Danny. I wondered if this difference in enthusiasm had anything to do with our ages. Medical research at the time indicated that the future prognosis for children with asthma was very bright, whereas for late-onset asthmatics, it was not good.

Thankfully, for about two years, the Quibron worked well.

After this, a definite pattern seemed to emerge. Attacks were rare in summer or mid-winter. The principal problem times were spring and autumn, and the most potent trigger factor was a sudden drop in temperature. Chest infections also caused asthma, and I was beginning to suspect an allergy to fish, because so many attacks occurred on our fish-eating Friday nights.

For some reason or other, I also developed asthma within two days of returning home from a holiday. Whether this was caused by the time of the year - March to April, or depression and tiredness from the effort of packing and unpacking plus huge amounts of washing, I don't know.

While the children were at primary school, we spent every holiday period at the Gold Coast. Jim, probably still hankering after his life-saving days, wouldn't consider going anywhere else. I couldn't face camping with small children, so we rented houses or units. Because rental fees double on the Gold Coast during peak seasons, we were forced to go either around February, March or November.

It was a drama writing to all the individual school teachers telling them we would be withdrawing the children from their classes for two weeks! Our kids worried about this, but, I don't think it did them any harm. Both Jim's and my parents stressed that a family must have a holiday away every year in order to maintain physical and mental health.

Holidaying in March probably meant we returned in time for the asthma season and that was why I always succumbed at that time.

When the Quibron ceased working, I visited our new doctor, who seemed very understanding. He prescribed Nuelin® tablets which were much more effective. The side-effects, however, were unpleasant; they made me feel shaky, and if taken after midnight caused headaches the following morning.

I joined a group of young mothers playing weekly squash. I really enjoyed this game because it afforded us all a chance to get together and indulge in adult conversation. As the squash courts had glass fronts and a play area for the toddlers, we could manage to have a happy sociable time while still keeping an eye on the children.

It became apparent, though, that unless I took a Nuelin® tablet the night before, I simply couldn't play the game; I had no energy. It appears that as I was getting older, my underlying condition was deteriorating.

Supermarkets were also a problem. How I hated those wide endless aisles with freezing air-conditioning. I did my best to avoid them and always sought out small, non-air-conditioned shops. When my favourite supermarket closed down, I was forced to frequent one of these chilly monsters. The only way I could cope with the weekly grocery order, was to leave the house about 11.30am, buy half the groceries, come home away from the air-conditioning for lunch, then head out again for the remainder of the shopping. I simply couldn't manage the distance around all the aisles — the further I pushed the trolley, the more difficult it was to breathe.

Most people would ask, 'Why didn't you take some medication before leaving home?' The fact is I didn't even think of it. Perhaps my upbringing had something to do with this. My mother had an abhorrence towards medication, and as children we practically had to write applications in triplicate for permission to take an aspirin.

Attending squash every week was evidently more important than shopping for groceries which I considered didn't warrant medication.

At age 36, I had been asthmatic for over seven years. Feeling guilty, I told few people of my condition. I think the adages of the sixties: 'Asthma is a psychosomatic disease' and 'An asthmatic child is an unloved child' haunted me. I had combined those opinions and arrived at the conclusion I was both neurotic and unlovable. Fortunately, because I didn't consider that I had chronic asthma, I could dismiss those thoughts most of the time — until a new pattern emerged.

During spring and autumn, a perpetual month-long tightening of the chest prevented me from inhaling a satisfying quantity of air. Oxygen deprivation brought with it perpetual fatigue and depression: none of the old 'it'll-all-be-over-in-two-days' feeling that I experienced with the more severe attacks. Nuelin® helped me sleep at night, but on the whole it didn't have much effect. Once the month was up, the asthma disappeared.

I began to wonder, when the twins started school, whether I would be able to participate in activities such as tuckshop. I felt my ill-health would make me too unreliable to make a commitment. On days when my asthma was more severe, I would thank God for television, sit the children in front of it and give myself a day in bed. The children enjoyed these days —when I was well, too much viewing was forbidden.

I virtually hybernated from the beginning of winter. At four every afternoon, in order to maintain a warm house, I closed every door and window. I rarely went out on cold nights and constantly had the heater on in the bedroom. Because the dreaded house-dust mite theory had replaced the psychosomatic label as a cause of asthma, I once drove myself into a cleaning frenzy, believing if I eradicated every speck of dust, I would be miraculously cured. It didn't work.

Various other triggers of asthma were soon being espoused — stress, pollen, changes in temperature, exercise, infection, reactions to cats and dogs etcetera. These 'causes' sounded feasible, except for the fact they all existed in the forties and fifties when the asthma rate was low. Obviously the triggers were just that; triggers. They could not have been the <u>cause</u> of asthma.

Confused, I was even beginning to dread the blooming of the beautiful flowering trees in our area.

Nothing remains the same, however, and future events were to bring about a dramatic alteration in my health and lifestyle. Strangely it was a near disaster which brought about this change.

BREAKTHROUGH

In my thirty-eighth year I was hospitalised with a 'virus'. My appendix ruptured — and an 'exploratory' operation led to an emergency appendectomy. Further complications: peritonitis, a blocked bowel, and gangrene kept me in hospital for another two weeks after the surgery. I remember waking at some ungodly hour every morning and thinking, 'How am I ever going to make it through the day?' But for the skill and dedication of an eminent Queensland surgeon, I would not be here. (Incidentally this tall impressive man was very slow to send his bill, and considering the extent of his involvement, his fee was minuscule.)

However, I digress, but I want to demonstrate how this traumatic episode actually produced some good because if I hadn't experienced that illness, I doubt I would have found my cure for asthma.

About eight weeks after this operation, I was deeply depressed because I had come down again with 'month-long asthma'. My disappointment was acute as it had taken me a full six weeks to recover, and here I was, mown down again. It all seemed very unfair (Looking back, I should have been grateful just to be alive).

Lying in bed one night, wheezing away and feeling sorry for myself, I suddenly pictured asthmatics all over the world, experiencing these same symptoms. I felt a strong empathy with them and vowed to do everything in my power to discover the cause of this illness.

It occurred to me that, having developed the disease in adulthood, I would be more likely to believe a cure was possible than a person suffering asthma from childhood. Surely long-term asthmatics would be more inclined to accept their disease as part of life.

I made a deal with God. 'You find me a cure for my asthma and I promise I'll publicise it in the hope it will help others.'

Now this is when amazing events occurred.

Only two days following this 'deal', Jim arrived home and related a conversation he had with a young co-worker, named Joy.

'How's Marian?' she asked.

'She's improved a lot since the operation,' said Jim, 'but now she's down with asthma.'

Joy replied, 'Asthma is a vitamin A deficiency. Marian needs more vitamin A, but it must be taken with vitamin E. I've heard paw-paw is supposed to be one of the best sources of vitamin A.'

When Jim relayed Joy's message, I believed in it immediately. I knew she was very interested in nutrition, and I'd experienced first-hand the benefits of vitamin A for bronchitis. Asthma did seem like a deficiency disease. It did appear to be systemic in that asthmatics often suffer other symptoms besides asthma such as: bronchitis, hay fever, rhinitis and eczema. I also remembered Jim telling me of a concept he called the 'trace element theory'. He said a farmer had shown him a field of wheat which was lovely and green except for one small patch, which was yellow. The farmer told Jim that the yellow wheat was growing in soil deficient in iron. A small sprinkle of iron in that section, would make the whole field green.

It occurred to me that vitamin A coul[d]
the missing 'trace element' in asthma —
similar to vitamin C in scurvy and iron in t[he]
wheat-field.

The following day I went out and bought
some vitamin A and synthetic E; natural E
wasn't available in those days. I hadn't a clue
what quantity to take, but considered if I had a
deficiency, one capsule would probably not be
sufficient, so I took two (total 10,000 units) and
one vitamin E (100 mg). I also increased my
consumption of foods containing vitamin A
and carotene, e.g. lamb's fry (not much I must
admit), cheese, eggs, carrots, paw-paw,
pumpkin, broccoli etcetera.

Within two days I felt marvellous; not a
sign of the chronic asthma which had dogged
me for the past fortnight. I was really excited
and contemplated ringing Joy immediately to
thank her for her advice. However, as the
whole thing seemed incredible and September
(usually a bad month for me) was looming, I
decided to wait three months before contacting
her.

Bliss.

Three months later and still no sign of
asthma.

I wasn't taking the vitamins every day, but
at the first sign of symptoms, took them
immediately and continued for a few days.

I tried to tell Joy of this wonderful improvement, only to discover she had left Jim's branch and her whereabouts were unknown. Luckily she rang Jim one day and he told her how thrilled I was with her cure.

Her reply surprised him. 'I didn't say asthma was a vitamin A deficiency,' she said. 'I said, most respiratory problems were a vitamin A deficiency. Asthma is supposed to be an allergy.'

I was shocked to hear Joy had not said asthma was a vitamin A deficiency. Jim however, stuck to his original version, maintaining he'd passed the message on correctly.

Well, I thought, what if someone did get their lines crossed and it was all a big mistake; it was a mistake in my favour and I wasn't about to abandon this new found treatment. I hadn't felt so well in years and was sleeping blissfully through the night with windows wide open. I was also back playing squash (requiring no medication), positively roaring around the supermarket and had completely dismissed all thoughts of the stupid house-dust mite. Evening barbeques were no longer avoided and nights out in town (instead of being fearful) were exciting once more.

I was liberated for the first time in ten years.

SETBACK

This new vitamin treatment was severely tested during the following particularly stressful year. My mother, who had sold her home, wanted to stay permanently with us. As our children ranged in ages from six to fifteen, I felt that adding an eighty-two-year-old to the home would make the situation too difficult.

This problem may not have pressured some people, but being an only daughter (who had never said 'No' to her mother) I found the stress to be intense. I didn't believe I might crack under the strain, I knew I would. Eventually, Jim came to the rescue and organised for Mum a lovely unit nearby where she lived happily until she died. My point here, though, is that in spite of several months of pressure, I had no symptoms of asthma. It seemed evident that the vitamins also counteracted severe stress.

<u>Three</u> years of excellent health followed. If I noticed a mild wheeze developing in the mornings, I would remind myself of the original premise, 'Asthma is a vitamin A deficiency' and simply increase the dose of A. This always worked. I was taking 15,000 units of vitamin A per day (one capsule after each meal) plus 100 mg of vitamin E. The vitamins usually took about twenty hours to take effect.

Everything went swimmingly until one April morning when at 3.00am I was wakened by a severe asthma attack. Stupidly, I'd allowed myself to run out of Nuelin® tablets, which meant hours of struggling for every breath. My rib-cage ached from the effort required to exhale. The next morning, feeling ill, debilitated and shaky, I visited our doctor for a repeat prescription of Nuelin®.

This set-back was devastating. My confidence in the vitamin A theory was shattered. I had not missed one dose of vitamins during the previous month. It was unbelievable. How could this happen after three asthma-free years? As any asthmatic will verify, to be free of asthma for 36 months, after suffering regularly for eight years, is nothing short of miraculous. Defeated, I asked myself, 'What was so different about that day from any other day?'

Could it have been the prawns we ate for tea? (as I said earlier, seafood seems to be a problem). But we'd eaten fish on other occasions with no ill effect. Could it have been the drop in temperature? But temperatures had dropped countless times over the past three years. Could it have been the 'too cold' air-conditioning at the shopping centre? But this hadn't altered either.

I was completely mystified.

It occurred to me that during the previous two weeks, I had been taking cod-liver oil capsules instead of my usual A (or A+D). I was under the impression that the cod-liver oil contained 5,000 units of vitamin A but on inspecting the bottle, I found it to be simply labelled '275 mg Cod Liver Oil'; no mention of the quantity of vitamin A and D in each capsule. In view of this ambiguity, I reverted to my usual capsules.

For the next six weeks, (periodically eating seafood) I felt fine. Then, considering it a waste not to use up the old capsules, I recommenced taking them. Ten days later, another severe attack — once more at 3.00am. This time I was certain the fault lay with the capsules; they must have been weaker than my usual type.

I rang the chemist at the vitamin company and was surprised when told these particular cod-liver oil capsules contained only 578 units of vitamin A — less than one eighth the usual strength.

What a relief!

My faith in the vitamins had been severely tested and I came close to failing the test.

I had almost considered giving up completely, but I resumed my normal dosage and another four years of asthma-free living followed.

During those years I found it necessary, during winter, to double the dose of vitamin A in order to maintain normal health. At age 42, I was taking 20,000 units of A, 200 mg of E and an occasional 500 mg of vitamin C. At age 44, 30,000 units of A were required and about 500 mg of E (in winter). During the summer months I reduced these amounts to almost nil.

On this regime, I experienced seven asthma-free years.

A surprising by-product of this treatment was the bonus of never again requiring nasal-drops. Previously a nasal-drop 'junkie' — 1980 was the last year it was necessary for me to purchase these drops. Hay fever attacks also were drastically reduced.

Another fact that amazed me throughout

these years, was that, although I succumbed to upper respiratory tract infections (URTI) with as much regularity as anyone else, these did not develop into asthma.

Many people believe that contracting a cold or influenza, while taking vitamins, automatically means the vitamins are not working. They then give up. Viral infections are unavoidable and while in the grip of them, in order to avoid asthma, we should be hitting the vitamins hard.

This is definitely not the time to quit.

PLUMBING THE DEPTHS

In 1984, I decided it was time to keep my end of the bargain made with God, and publicise my cure. *The Sunday Mail* published my letter to the editor and gave it top billing. The huge number of phone calls that followed completely overwhelmed me. All callers were inquiring about the dosage I used.

The dozens of callers demonstrated that they were disillusioned with the drug approach to asthma. If the reverse occurred and a fellow asthmatic wrote a letter extolling the virtues of a new asthma drug, I wouldn't bother ringing him or her, as nothing could surpass the vitamin approach.

As a result of this publicity, there were soon ten of us achieving excellent results using vitamins to control our asthma.

I don't know how the other callers fared, however, because although they all said they would report on their progress, very few did. This puzzled me, but after hearing the reactions from doctors, relatives and friends, I understood why so many were afraid to try the vitamins.

The mother of a sixteen-year-old asthmatic said, 'When I asked the doctor if there was anything more natural my daughter could try, he replied, "Do you want her to die?".' Later this same mother watched another doctor administer so much salbutamol to her daughter, that the girl lost consciousness.

Another asthma sufferer, after informing his doctor of his intention to take vitamins, was told, 'Vitamins don't work! That medical matriarch (refering to Lady Cilento and her book *Medical Mother*) who pushes them all the time, is a quack. The only reason she's lived so long is longevity runs in her family.'

The strangest and most unbelievable comment I heard attributed to a health professional was 'Vitamins can damage your lungs.' This was told to the mother of a four-

year-old asthmatic who attended a
kindergarten in Ipswich where thirteen of the
twenty-five pre-schoolers suffered asthma.

Friends and relatives also discouraged
many with their 'Vitamin A is poisonous'
theory. I considered this absolutely ridiculous.
How could a vitamin be poisonous?

Lady Cilento (*Medical Mother* p86) writes:
*'This cry of "toxic" by the American FDA
and our own echo of the same label have caused
many consumers to avoid vitamin A and may
have caused serious deficiencies among consumers of all ages. The labelling of "toxic" is
now silenced by order of the Federal Court in
US, and I only hope that the Australian
Health Department will follow suit.'*

In view of these scare tactics, it is easy to
understand why so many asthmatics were
frightened.

Still there were nine brave souls who
continued the vitamin treatment. Ironically,
Joy, the catalyst of this vitamin theory, married
a young man who was a severe asthmatic. He
also improved amazingly. Now there were ten
of us thrilled by our good health.

Curiosity as to why vitamin A worked so
well for asthma prompted me to do some

research. One day I found a publication entitled *Improving Your Health with Vitamin A* by Ruth Adams and Frank Murray.

This book contained many chapters about the use of vitamin A as a cancer preventative.

'Vitamin A for cancer?' I thought. 'Whatever will they come up with next?' Of course, recent medical research has indicated vitamin A could be a preventative for some cancers, particularly of the lungs and breast. However at that time, I was prepared to dismiss the authors as a pair of crackpots. One section, though, did look interesting — the list of various functions which vitamin A performed in the body, such as: Vitamin A is needed for the health of the eyes, for night vision, colour, and side vision, for healthy linings of all body openings and organs, for resistance to infection, for bone development, to maintain the adrenal glands and the synthesis of certain hormones.

Three of these functions of vitamin A are of particular interest to asthmatics, namely:

1. Resistance to infection.

2. Maintenance of linings of the lungs.

3. Maintenance of adrenal glands and synthesis of   certain hormones.

Surely the lungs would be more sensitive

to irritants and infection if the linings were not maintained well, and as for the adrenal glands, which hormones did they produce I wondered?

No doubt adrenalin would be one. I knew some asthmatics received injections of adrenalin and that drugs such as salbutamol imitated the action of adrenalin. Wouldn't the adrenal glands produce less adrenalin if they too were run down through lack of vitamin A?

Investigating the subject, I discovered two of the principal hormones produced by the adrenal glands, were adrenalin and cortisone. I was excited by this information. (Don't forget we didn't study biology during my school days.) I knew cortisone was given to asthmatics so it occurred to me that maybe a shortage of vitamin A could also mean a shortage of cortisone.

I was so excited that I woke Jim up to tell him about it.

'Come on Marian,' he said. 'If you can work that out so can the doctors. If they knew vitamin A worked they would be giving it to their patients.'

'Maybe they don't believe it would work, so they haven't even tried it. I've tried it and I know it works.'

I became even more interested in the

study of vitamin A after this, and asked our eldest son, Danny, who was studying Science at Queensland University, to bring home some books from the library.

In one publication *Biochemical Basis of Medicine*, by E.D. Wills, it was demonstrated that rats which were fed diets deficient in vitamin A, were found to have lowered levels of natural cortisone in their bodies. (There didn't appear to be any studies on humans.) If rats are a reliable indicator, how many people are struggling to survive with low levels of cortisone? It appears many of us are deficient in vitamin A.

I found evidence of this in my second, less judgmental reading of *Improving Your Health with Vitamin A*. It described an examination of 500 autopsy specimens, from five different cities in Canada, which revealed that over 30 per cent of the cadavers had less vitamin A in their livers than when they were born. Eight specimens from Ottawa and 20 per cent from Montreal, showed no vitamin A stores at all.

The ages ranged from stillborn to ninety-two, with the majority being over fifty.

Dr T. Keith Murray, when reporting these facts to a nutrition congress held in August, 1968, at Puerto Rico, said 'It is hard to blame diet alone. Even allowing for wastage, cooking losses etcetera it does not seem likely that so many of our population do not get enough vitamin A to maintain their reserves.'

Canadian experts believed there must be something in our environment which is causing us to use up more vitamin A than we can consume, or else our liver stores of vitamin A are being attacked by some substance.

These people suspected pesticides.

Did they suspect pesticides because both pesticides and vitamin A are fat soluble, and both accumulate in the liver? (Australians would have higher pesticide levels than Americans because we still use chemicals banned years ago in America.)

If pesticides or some other chemicals are killing off our vitamin A supplies, or causing us to use up more than we can consume, or preventing absorption of this vitamin, then this could explain why supplementing our diet with extra vitamin A has such a dramatic effect.

To summarise my theory:

Adrenal glands need vitamin A to keep them healthy and help produce cortisone.

Cortisone is needed in the lungs to reduce inflammation (one of the chief problems in asthma).

Pesticides or some other substances are affecting our vitamin A stores.

If we are suffering from asthma we undoubtedly have insufficient vitamin A to produce enough cortisone.

With regards to pesticides — when we consider that humans are at the top of the food chain, the amount of pesticides and heavy metals that we collect in our bodies, is magnified many times. Most pesticides and heavy metals require lengthy periods to fully break down, so each animal or plant that we consume will probably still contain these poisons in its system. As we consume large quantities of all these living products, we naturally absorb large amounts of poisons.

The quantity of food additives present in today's processed foods, and absent from our ancestors' diets, should also be considered as possible destroyers of vitamin A. Are we sure these chemicals are completely safe? Are we certain they are not destroying vitamins or causing us to require more?

Authors, Ross Meillon and Chris Reading claim that many vitamin deficiencies are caused by allergies to food. They claim food allergies prevent the absorption of vitamins. (*Relatively Speaking* p.100). Could this factor also be affecting asthmatics?

Another theory for low levels of vitamin A in our livers, was mentioned in *The Complete Book of Vitamins*. Dr R.J. Emerick of South Dakota State College proved that nitrites (which form nitrogen from fertilisers and which appears in our plant food and water supplies) destroyed raw carotene — the precursor of vitamin A, while in an environment similar to the stomach.

Other contributors to *The Complete Book of Vitamins* have more to say on the subject. The U.S. Army Research Institute of Environmental Medicine, testing on rats, proved that when the temperature drops, the body uses less of the available vitamin A and stores more away.

I can't understand why nature dictates the liver should grab so much vitamin A right when we need it. Maybe it's stockpiled for an anticipated attack of winter influenza?

These researchers also stated:

'As the weather gets colder, the consumption of vitamin A should increase to help maintain the same level of health during the winter as in the warmer months.'

When we consider this information on pesticides, herbicides, food additives and fertilisers and accept that they all increased enormously after World War II, it does seem that a connection can reasonably be made between these factors and the incredible increase in asthma since that time.

Whatever the cause of this vitamin deficiency my belief is this:

Asthma is a vitamin A deficiency.

Vitamin A must always be taken with vitamin E (to protect the A) and some vitamin C is usually required as well.

Of course, the most common response from those hearing this theory for the first time, is 'You shouldn't go around saying things like that. Just because vitamin A works for you, doesn't mean it will work for everyone.'

My answer to this is 'It doesn't only work for me; it works for many others as well and why shouldn't it work for everyone?' Where has it ever been demonstrated that vitamin C will cure scurvy in some, but not in others?

Who ever heard vitamin B12 only occasionally controls pernicious anaemia? The same could be said for the other diseases controlled by vitamins:

Rickets - Vitamin D; Pellagra - Vitamin B3; Beriberi - Vitamin B1.

Admittedly, most of these diseases are seldom seen in Australia, but pernicious anaemia is common (I personally know of six cases, who adhere to healthy diets). The point is, we do not have to live in a third world country to be deficient in a vitamin. Regarding asthma, though, I believe the only reason vitamin A might not work for 'everyone' is simply that 'everyone' hasn't tried it. As previously stated, I've never known this treatment to fail, if adhered to correctly.

I once spoke of this vitamin treatment to a woman involved in fundraising for childhood diseases. Her reaction surprised me.

'I don't want you to take this the wrong way, dear, but I don't think anyone is going to believe in that theory of yours.'

'Why not?'

'Well,' she said, 'it's just too simple.'

She seemed a very kind person so I didn't labour the point, but as a good friend of mine said, 'Some of the world's greatest discoveries have been very simple.'

Because asthma has become such a complicated disease, some people find it impossible to believe a simple approach would have any effect. I believe it's a mistake to think like that. Scurvy was once considered one of the biggest killers of all time, and look how that was dealt with.

As far as asthma is concerned, we should also remember that there are drug companies with vested interests. Would they want to know of a simple treatment for this disease?

It is important for those of us who have found relief with this 'too simple approach' to hold fast to our belief, and refuse to back down under the pressure.

Eventually we will win.

HOPING FOR CLINICAL RESEARCH

In 1985, I decided that clinical research into my ideas was essential. I rang two hospitals' university departments to inquire if any one was researching asthma. I quickly retreated from the first contact. His name was listed on the Asthma Foundation's medical advisory board. Of course the Asthma Foundation is a marvellous help to asthmatics, but all my communications to the board had been completely ignored. Eventually, with the help of a senior staff member of the Asthma Foundation, I did receive one letter which was addressed, not to me, but to him. He kindly forwarded that letter which stated, 'Recommending treatments such as vitamin A and E could jeopardise people's lives because asthmatics might neglect their usual medication.'

I couldn't understand why the writer would think such a thing. Everyone knows if an asthmatic was to suddenly cease his or her medication, it could be life threatening.

Why couldn't asthma sufferers, while still retaining their drugs, be encouraged to increase their intake of vitamins A and E without that being deemed to 'jeopardise lives'?

Feeling distinctly apathetic towards the Asthma Foundation following their dismissive letter, I managed to contact a researcher not attached to the board, and asked if I could show him the case histories of the ten asthmatics using vitamins. He was very kind and agreed to see me.

Nervous about the impending interview, I hastily gathered and collated the case histories. Jim, probably in an attempt to bring me down to earth, said, 'Don't get yourself in a flap. He'll probably grab the file and say, "Thanks a lot. Here's yer hat; so what's yer hurry"?'

By the time I arrived for the meeting I'd convinced myself Jim was right, so I was amazed at being immediately ushered into the doctor's room and offered coffee and biscuits. How I wished I'd thought a little more about what I wanted to say to this tall, cultured gentleman whose kind attitude made conversation easy.

I was surprised that a doctor would actually take my ideas seriously. Until then I hadn't met one who was so open to unorthodox theories. Perhaps his interest in vitamin A had been aroused by a research article he showed me about rats which had been severely burnt and were subsequently treated with 3,000 units of vitamin A. Evidently the treatment was successful. I thought to myself 'What's this got to do with the price of eggs?'

Seeing my perplexity, he explained, 'You know that the lungs are badly affected in burn cases?'

I didn't know this, but all I could think to say was, '3,000 units is an awful lot of vitamin A for a rat!'

He read my files, expressed interest in carrying out research, and proceeded to tell me how 'we' could do it.

'Preliminary tests would have to be done first, and the actual research would involve double-blind trials extending over a period of four years. An ethics committee would have to approve the experiment before any work could begin,' he said.

Carried away with the idea, I happily agreed to assist with the research.

On arriving home reality hit me. How could I find the time to help anyone when I still had six dependant children? Regretfully, I contacted the doctor and outlined my problem. He, in turn was having second thoughts about the professionalism of using anyone below the status of a Ph.D. student. Such a student, working for four years would cost in the vicinity of $70,000 (over $80,000 today I would imagine). He said, 'That kind of money isn't available at the moment.'

When I expressed hopelessness about the whole project, he said, 'Don't be so pessimistic. The University sometimes receives bequests for research.' I offered any clerical help I could with the future research, but unfortunately that day has not yet arrived.

So, if you are rich and have thousands to spare, think about bequeathing it to the Queensland University for research into Vitamin A for Asthma!

SUCCESS STORIES OF OTHER ASTHMATICS

Here is some of the material I presented to the doctor, plus a few recent case studies.

Various asthmatics living in the Brisbane and nearby coastal areas who have found success with the use of vitamins, have kindly signed statements in the hope that research might eventually be carried out (These names have been changed to protect privacy).

As you will see, this vitamin approach works for an eighty-year-old woman as well as a twelve-year-old-boy. Both men and women seem to experience success, so no one need say

'It might work for others, but it couldn't work for me.'

CASE STUDIES

Marie — Aged 80, A Lifetime Asthmatic

This amazing lady rang after seeing my letter in the paper. She told me she had accidentally discovered the same 'cure' for her asthma as I had for mine.

An asthmatic from birth, she began taking multi-vitamins in 1941. Some years later she developed a chronic throat problem and persuaded her doctor to prescribe 20,000 units of vitamin A. Because it controlled her problem so well, she continued with the vitamin A.

When she was seventy-eight she inquired of Lady Phyllis Cilento, whether she was taking the correct vitamins for her age.

Lady Cilento said everything was fine, except she needed much more vitamin E. She was told to <u>gradually</u> increase her E to 750 mgs daily.

Marie did as she was told, and found to her amazement that her asthma disappeared. She told me she'd had no symptoms of asthma during the previous three years. I asked her if she would sign a statement for me, but she said 'No, I don't want my name bandied around the University.'

In 1988, Marie rang back to say she had changed her mind and would like to be included when clinical research is conducted.

Darren - Aged 41, Forced to Give up Jogging

(Copy of Letter)
20th Sept, 1985.
Dear Marian,
I refer to your previous letter concerning the use of vitamins in the treatment of asthma. I am most pleased to provide the following information:

1. In 1983 I had cause to visit my doctor because it appeared I had developed an asthmatic problem. The symptoms were brought on by exercise; I enjoy jogging and other forms of exercise. Secondly as the evening approached my chest would 'tighten' and my breathing would be mainly to and from the top of my lungs.

2. My doctor prescribed Bricanyl® and Becotide® which I regularly (each day) blew into my mouth.

3. I was somewhat concerned that at the age of 41, I was relying on this form of medication.

4. A friend of ours advised me of a treatment

she had read about for the type of complaint from which I was suffering. (I should say the problem was not a major one but it was uncomfortable at times and the discomfort appeared to be worsening.) I had to give up my regular jogging.

5. The treatment I then followed (and still do religiously) involved the taking of vitamins A, E and C. I also take one aspirin per day on my doctor's advice to assist in keeping my blood thinner than it would be otherwise.

6. I commenced this procedure in 1983 and have had no asthma problems since. In fact in 1983, 84 and this year I ran as linesman around the boundary for my son's Australian Rules football team and can jog for an hour or more with no breathing problems. The cold evening air no longer has any adverse effect on my breathing.

I trust that this information is of assistance to you. Should the researcher wish to talk with me about my use of vitamins, I would be pleased to meet with him.

Best wishes in your endeavours,

Yours sincerely,

(Darren).

Janine - Aged 35, Acute Asthmatic

(Copy of letter)
24th June, 1985.
Dear Marian,

A few notes I hope will put you in the picture.

I had my first attack of asthma at 28 years of age in 1978. We had just moved to Rockhampton. At that time it didn't seem severe and was able to be controlled with Ventolin® and Becotide®.

We moved back to our present address in 1981 and the asthma seemed a little worse. In early 1982, after cleaning up plaster dust in our new home, I developed a severe attack and was in hospital for nine days. After that, my asthma was less easily controlled and resulted in several trips to hospital for a few days. When I had an attack, Ventolin® seemed useless.

I read your article (S.M. August 5th, 1984). My last attack of asthma was in June, 1984. I took cortisone at home during that time.

I mainly seemed to get asthma with a cold. Last year the specialist suggested I try having the 'flu shot to see if it would help. I did and also had it again this year.

Since I have been taking the vitamins, I have weaned myself off taking Ventolin® and Becotide® regularly, but haven't let the Theodur® go yet.

During danger times, e.g. when I have a cold, I

take l (10,000 i.u.) vitamin A; (100 mg) vitamin E and 1 Theodur® morning and night. Other times I take 1 A, 1 E and half a Theodur® in the morning and an E and half Theodur® at night.

I have woken some mornings feeling a little tight, used Ventolin®, stepped up the A and not developed an attack.

Marian, although I am not strictly on just vitamins, I feel that they have helped greatly. So far, at least I seem to be a little in control and I would like to get away from the cortisone, drips etc. for good. I have told my doctor what I am doing in case I have a severe attack. The specialist does not know as I have not had cause to see him since starting the vitamins. He did say I had acute asthma.

I wish a qualified person could look into this. I have tried what you suggested in your article, I feel so much better, and I am very thankful you took the time and effort to write it.

Kindest regards,

(Janine).

Janine has contacted me every Christmas since. She continued with the vitamins for nearly six years during which time she kept extremely well. In 1989, however, she informed me she had ceased taking the vitamins because she had been told they caused kidney damage. After ceasing the vitamins, she developed very severe asthma and eventually visited a naturopath who suggested she eat six carrots every morning plus plenty of fresh nuts. Her last Christmas card said she had a very good year.

(I would like to mention here, that I have never heard or read that vitamins A or E cause kidney damage. I did read of a case of an elderly man, dying of kidney failure who was given a large dose of vitamin C and when the autopsy was carried out, the vitamin C was found crystallised in his kidneys. I don't know whether the stories of kidney damage came from that case, but if they did, it's not a very good example — the man was dying at the time!)

Janine seems very happy with her current dietary approach to her asthma. She wrote, Christmas 1993, that she was still keeping well. She said she had eased up considerably with the carrot juice, taking it mainly when she catches a cold.

Brendan — Aged 12
(Extract from File)

Brendan developed asthma at nine years of age. He often had to cease playing basketball because of nausea. He was on Becotide®, Theodur® and Ventolin®.

July 1988 — Brendan commenced the vitamins. He managed to forgo the Becotide® and Theodur® in the first week. His mother said there was an amazing improvement. She said his colour was much better and whereas in the past he always woke at 5.30 or 6.00am, coughing and wheezing, after commencing the vitamins, she had to wake him every morning. During the first month he used his Ventolin® only a couple of times.

December 1988 — Five months have elapsed since Brendan began the vitamins. His father said he had only required his Ventolin® puffer a couple of times in the last few months. He added that his son was playing lots of sport and both parents were very impressed with his improvement.

Brendan is taking about 10,000 units of vitamins A and 100 mg E.

October 1991 — Rang Brendan's mother. She said he had been keeping well, although he doesn't take the vitamins regularly. He plays two games of basketball every weekend and sometimes uses his puffer before play. He is sleeping well and she believes the vitamins are responsible for his improved health. He no longer suffers nausea when playing sport.

Narelle — Aged 12, Developed Asthma at 11

Narelle's mother rang in August 1988 to say that Narelle had developed asthma twelve months previously. She was using a Ventolin® puffer most of the time and taking two Nuelin® tablets a day as well.

<u>December 1988</u> — Since beginning the vitamins (10,000 units A and 100 mg E) four months ago, Narelle has hardly used her puffer. She was also off the Nuelin®. Her mother said something which stays in my mind:

'If they invented a drug as good as this, it would be hailed as a wonder drug. Isn't it a pity so few know about it?'

<u>October 1991</u> — Rang Narelle's mother. She said Narelle had been keeping very well and she believed the vitamins were mainly responsible for her daughter's improved health.

Leeanne — aged 5

Leeanne began the vitamins in <u>June 1988</u>. During the first month she developed a throat infection, followed by a chest infection. However, there was no asthma with either. Leeanne's mother was amazed by this.

<u>March 1989</u> — *Husband, Jim, who works with Leeanne's father, was informed Leeanne was keeping very well. Leeanne is taking about 5,000 units of vitamin A per day and 100 mg of E every second day.*

John — Aged 44, Collapsed on Way to Work

<u>November 1986</u> — *John rang and told me he had developed asthma at 43 years of age. He was walking to work one morning, when he simply collapsed. He woke in the hospital and was quite surprised when told he had suffered a severe asthma attack.*

He began taking vitamins A and E and said he was about 80% improved.

<u>February 1988</u> — *John rang again to tell me he was still on the vitamins and doing well.*

Elizabeth — Aged 53, Doctor recommended cigarettes as a treatment for nerves of the stomach in 1955

(Copy of Letter)
June 12, 1994
Dear Marian,
Having been a smoker for thirty-nine years and having "sludge-pump" lungs to prove it, I

think I'm a good advertisement for your vitamin theory, Marian.

Briefly, I developed bronchial asthma in my late thirties, and was loathe to use the puffers prescribed; they interfered with my smoking. I did, however, take the Nuelin® when it was needed and used the Ventolin® only when I needed to breathe. My doctor despaired.

Time means little to me, but I think I seriously began taking vitamins A and E about a year ago.

Recently, after weeks of URTI, I went to my doctor expecting the usual lecture, and was amazed when it didn't eventuate. I think you'll appreciate the following conversation:

'So,' he said, 'you've given up the smokes at last.'

'No.'

'You've cut them down a lot then?'

'No.'

'Get away with you. Patients come in here vowing they've stopped. You have and you're not admitting it.'

'I'm not lying,' said I with a grin.

'All right, what's the story?'

'I'm smoking as much as, if not more than before —

but I've been taking vitamin A.'

I forgot to mention the E, Marian. Anyway, I paused, waiting for the usual 'People who eat properly, don't need vitamins...', but he said nothing.

'Go on, rubbish the vitamins,' I baited him.

'I can't.' He looked pitifully confused. 'Beth, I've never known your lungs to be so clear.'

I confessed that I hardly ever used the puffers anyway, but had continued to take Nuelin®. He updated my records by deleting the puffers from the 'current medication' list.

Thanks to you, Marian, I have been 'certified' as being the healthiest I've been in years, despite the URTI. I must admit, though, that I don't take much care with dosage. I swallow from 10,000 to 40,000 units of Vitamin A and 500 units of E depending on how I feel.

Marian, I am truly grateful to you for telling me about the vitamins.

I remain,
Healthfully yours,
Elizabeth.

There are twenty-five cases on file. All have reported considerable improvement.

VITAMIN FILLERS

An article outlining my case history was published in 1985 by the Allergy Association, (Newsletter Issue No. 10). It surprised me because my article concentrated on vitamins rather than allergies, however the connection made me consider my proneness to allergies.

Asthmatics prefer to live in a fresh, plain, rather old-fashioned environment. Twentieth century inventions such as hair-spray, fly-spray, herbicides, petrol fumes, paint fumes etcetera, often cause distress. We become adept at finding ways to avoid these irritants, but I'm sure I speak for the majority when I say the most difficult of all to avoid is cigarette smoke.

Some smokers are extremely considerate. They always sit near open windows and doors when visiting and, if smoking while driving, will hold their cigarette near the window of the car. These smokers do not upset me, although some brands of cigarettes are worse than others.

The most maddening smokers are those people who hold their cigarette right under your face. Smouldering cigarette smoke always gives me a runny nose and/or a dry cough.

My friend said, 'I agree with you. Some smokers are inconsiderate, but my worst irritant is strong perfumes. My doctor told me that perfume induced asthma attacks can actually be life threatening? Imagine being stuck next to a highly perfumed person on a long distance flight. You can't escape in elevators either. In this 'politically correct' environment, where smokers are denied their rights for the good of our health, should not the wearing of strong perfumes/aftershaves also be banned in public places.

Perfumed pages in magazines and the salespeople of those scents who insist on squirting offensive substances as you pass their display counter, are another pet hate. One can hardly shower and change clothes while shopping.'

Her statement caused me to wonder if these products are ever tested on 'sensitive' people before they are released? If not, they should be.

As well as enduring respiratory irritation, we asthmatics also tend to be sensitive to skin irritants. I exercise considerable care in my choice of detergents, toilet soaps, make-up and even toothpaste. The twentieth century has not been kind to asthmatics.

Which brings me to internal allergies. Many people find they have a lack of tolerance to many foods. In my case, apart from seafood, I've not found that foods cause asthma. Certain foods, however, do cause abdominal distress. My list includes red wine, chocolate, vegemite, wheat germ, some brands of cheese, lemon grass, and some orange coloured vitamin C tablets. (I've recently discovered that many of these foods belong to a category which nutritionists call 'The Amines.' Three quarters of our family suffers some type of reaction to these foods.)

As my abdominal reaction takes several hours to manifest and the symptoms then persist for up to two days, it was a mammoth task isolating the offending substances — only a stubborn woman such as I would even try. (Seriously, though, I think most would attempt to track down these allergens; they tend to cause depression along with the abdominal distress.)

My nutritionist says many emotional problems can be traced to food allergies.

The most successful detection method I've found is to maintain a diary of symptoms; particularly noting the 'good days' and what was different about them. This usually pin-points the culprit fairly quickly.

A woman at an Allergy Association meeting said something which remains in my memory. She was speaking to the mother of a small, very allergy-prone girl. 'I feel so sorry for your child.' she said. 'It has taken me a lifetime to discover all the things I'm allergic to.'

I'm sure many asthmatics could relate to that.

Which brings me to one of my pet gripes — vitamin fillers. Why do vitamin companies persist in using allergy producing ingredients as fillers for their vitamin tablets? No one can be allergic to a vitamin, but they certainly can be allergic to the fillers used. How many times do we hear people say, 'Vitamins? No, I can't take them. They give me indigestion,' or some other intestinal reaction.

The first time I experienced an abdominal

reaction from a vitamin supplement, I thought I'd developed some deadly disease. The discomfort lasted three weeks before I finally suspected the orange coloured vitamin C powder I was using. I mean, vitamins are the last thing you would expect to make you sick!

Some vitamin companies are very aware of allergy problems and ensure that their products contain low-allergy ingredients. Many companies simply don't care.

It amazes me any health product should ever contain allergenic ingredients. It's even more incongruous when we consider that those most likely to require vitamin supplements, are the very people who are prone to allergic reactions.

In their book (*Relatively Speaking* P.100) Ross Meillon and Chris Reading claim, in relation to diet, that 'allergies cause inability to absorb vitamins.'. This is a very interesting concept and could explain why so many people, like myself who suffer food allergies, seem to require more vitamins than others.

We can only guess at the number of asthmatics who have been discouraged for life from using vitamins, simply because they were unfortunate enough to purchase a vitamin brand which contained something to which they were allergic. This is tragic.

It is simply not good enough to state 'Low Allergy — contains no (this or that).' What help is that if a person's allergen is not printed on the bottle? It's time all manufacturers were legally forced to list every ingredient in their product. With so many people allergic to a variety of substances, it is dangerous to keep them in ignorance. There has been an enormous improvement in the labelling of foodstuffs on supermarket shelves; lists of ingredients are found on most labels. Let us hope that vitamin companies will soon follow suit.

Listed below are some recommendations for the purchase of vitamins:

1. Buy direct from the distributor. It's cheaper.

2. Buy only fresh vitamins (this is particularly important in the case of natural vitamin E).

3. Buy only vitamins which are 'Low Allergy'. Even then you may have to experiment to find fillers that fully agree with you.

ASTHMA TREATMENTS ARE TOO COMPLICATED

Along with other sufferers and parents, I attended an asthma seminar in 1986 conducted by a doctor. The information shared at that gathering was both disturbing and enlightening.

In one instance, a mother's anger overflowed when the lecturer told of a death in a hospital ward.

'A nine-year-old boy died,' said the doctor, 'because of the stress caused by his estranged parents arguing over who was to take him home for the holiday break.'

'Are you blaming the parents for his death?' the woman snapped, 'How come he died in hospital with every treatment available?'

The lecturer quickly changed the subject.

A dark-haired young man, sitting near the front, leapt to his feet and demanded that future doctors be trained to 'please please listen to mothers.'

Another woman told how her child had been on Intal® to prevent asthma and she had suffered as many attacks on the drug, as off it.

When asked, 'What does asthma mean to you?' an attractive, but obviously tired, middle-aged woman stood up and said: 'Asthma means poverty to me. We have <u>six</u> asthmatics in our family.'

Here was a tall, burly doctor standing in front of a table laden with pharmaceutical products. Never have I seen so many medications and accessories for one disease! Could some of the anger in that room be attributed to fear of commercial exploitation?

Similar feelings surface when we observe the reactions of medical practitioners to any natural approach to asthma. The simpler treatment is either dismissed with a laugh or a warning is issued on the dire consequences of following anything but the orthodox line.

Everyone knows drugs are sometimes essential in asthma, but surely simple, natural and safer methods should always be tried first, especially where small children are concerned.

Any housewife will agree that to remove a stain from a garment, you begin with gentle treatments to avoid damaging the fabric; severe methods are only tried when everything else has failed. Why is this not done with asthma? Why do we find four-year-olds on cortisone?

A pharmaceutical salesman told me he often put the following question to doctors, 'Would you give steroids to your four-year-old?'

The orthodox treatment for asthma demands too much of the patient and too much of the general practitioner. Some asthmatics are taking up to forty puffs of one medication or another every day. How do they cope?

The problem is, should anything go wrong, it is too easy to blame the patient for not remembering to take all his or her medicine; the parent for neglecting to give it to the child or even the doctor for not stressing the importance of each medication.

Surely there could be nothing more painful than to be blamed for the death or severe illness of a loved one. It would be similar to blaming parents when a child drowns in a swimming pool. Haven't those parents suffered enough? It is absolutely <u>criminal</u> to inflict blame on grieving relatives.

The huge amounts of medication some asthmatics are taking must interfere with their quality of life. A mother told me her thirteen-year-old son was unable to sit for a technical drawing exam because his hands were still trembling from the nebuliser he'd used that morning.

A good friend, Beverley, described another case. Her lively little four-year-old niece, who was very proud of her ability to tie bows, offered to demonstrate this art for her aunt. However, she was unable to tie the ribbon because her hands were shaking too much. Like the thirteen-year-old boy, this tot had also been attached to a nebuliser. Beverley said, 'It was very sad to hear the child say, "Sometimes I can't do it, Aunty.".'

(Imagine the out-cry if vitamin A caused side-effects like that!)

Lately the trend seems to be more towards inhaled cortisone as a preventative, and away from bronchodilators. While the dangers of over-exposure to bronchodilators are receiving more attention, the belief in the safety of inhaled cortisone is dubious and will probably be resisted by concerned users who have heard of the detrimental effects of long-term cortisone use.

The medical profession is not infallible. When I was growing up in Central Queensland, I asked my mother why the nurses from the local hospital were practically the only women in the town who smoked cigarettes. My mother replied that the doctors encouraged the nurses to smoke because it was good for their nerves.

I found that difficult to believe. Surely no doctor would encourage smoking? It was common knowledge that cigarettes were addictive and I'm sure the term 'smoker's cough' was well known. Admittedly, at that time, no one knew anything of the fatal side-effects.

When a person deals constantly with sickness, does he or she lose interest in maintaining natural good health? The man who discovered vitamin C, Dr Albert Szent-Györgyi seemed to feel this could be a problem:

'Present medicine is lop-sided. As a medical student I had to listen no end to lectures on disease, but cannot remember one on health, full health!' (Vitamin C Against Cancer *Dr Szent-Györgyi) won a Nobel Prize in 1937.*

As to the inhaled cortisone question, I don't pretend to understand the medical aspect. All I know is that when I asked my doctor many years ago for a repeat of cortisone cream for my hands, he asked me how long I'd been using it.

I said 'On and off for thirteen years.'

He replied, 'You can't keep using that forever, you know.' (Present day opinion is even more conservative.)

What puzzles me is this. If it's not safe to continue using cortisone on my hands, why would it be safe to keep pumping it into my lungs?

REACTIONS FROM HEALTH PROFESSIONALS

By 1987, Danny (aged twenty-one) and I had been using the vitamins for eight years. During that time, neither he nor I experienced chronic asthma or any acute attacks (apart from the episode with the ultra-weak cod-liver-oil dosage). It was amazing how healthy we were. I found I could also tolerate very small quantities of seafood, and chocolate, which I'd been avoiding for years.

Sometimes in winter (particularly the month of June) I increased my vitamin A to

30,000 units — three capsules each 10,000 units. To balance this, during summer, I greatly reduced all vitamin intake. Danny stayed with the 10,000 units of A and 200 mg of E (when he remembered to take it!) We also took vitamin C if we caught colds. The total vitamin dose was divided into two or three with the capsules taken after meals. We experienced no side-effects whatsoever.

Often I marvelled at my good fortune. What a blessing to be able to cope with tuckshop rosters, Safety House Committees, the making of ballet costumes, school uniforms and formal dresses, parent-teacher interviews etcetera - I would never have managed all this plus squash and the occasional outing with Jim had I not discovered the benefits of vitamins A and E. I'd have felt perpetually tired and tormented. Occasionally, when purchasing new vitamins, I would be warned to be careful. I remember the words of one young lady chemist, 'These vitamins are accumulative, you know; you could have a reaction. Have you been taking them for long?'

'I've been taking them for seven years now,' I said, 'and if I suffered a major reaction tonight, it would all be worth-while, because I've had seven asthma-free years.' Afterwards, I wished I'd reminded her that any reaction is completely reversible upon cessation of the vitamin. Most health professionals seem to forget that fact, or maybe they simply do not know it.

It seemed I was forever being warned of the dangers of vitamins.

I could understand this if the orthodox approach to asthma was one hundred percent successful but all the asthmatics I'd spoken to over the years, were on at least two types of medication and were still suffering symptoms.

Surely the fact that they rang me demonstrated how unhappy they were on medication.

Nurses who were trained in the fifties (or thereabouts) have said they were taught that alternative medicine was 'pure quackery and no notice must be taken of it whatsoever'.

If alternative medicine is quackery, does this mean that the champion of the vitamin cause, Dr Linus Pauling, the only person to win two Nobel Prizes and acclaimed the world's greatest chemist, is a quack?

Whenever a cure from vitamins is reported, the usual response is 'Oh, that's only the placebo effect.' Anyone would think it an obscenity to discuss the concept that vitamins can alleviate so serious a disease as asthma. Captain Cook must have triggered some strange reactions when he stated, to prevent scurvy, he was packing limes and pickled vegetables aboard his ship. And Lady Cilento wrote that scurvy was one of the most feared killer diseases of all time, claiming more victims than the plague.

Actually the placebo effect has no influence on the outcome of the vitamin approach. Most of us who use vitamins for asthma, are absolutely amazed that they work at all.

One of the most peculiar responses I received when speaking of vitamins, came from a Community Health Nurse. We had finished listening to a two-hour lecture on asthma and countless types of medication. I mentioned the benefits of vitamins A and E to the group and the nurse retorted, 'You shouldn't go around saying things like that. Some young people would go out and buy a bottle of vitamin A and swallow the whole lot!'

I expressed utter disbelief at this, but she assured me she definitely knew what she was talking about. Since then, other professionals (chiefly chemists) have said the same thing.

Why the exaggerated concern that someone might swallow a whole bottle of vitamin A? I've attended many lectures about numerous asthma medications, but never once was any fear expressed that anyone might swallow an entire bottle of prescribed tablets.

This is amazing when you consider that a report released in 1992 by the then Federal Health Minister, Mr Staples, claimed more than 900 lives are lost per year, from the over-use (chiefly among the elderly) of prescription drugs.

Surely this is what we should all be concerned about. Why the 'hang-up' with nutritional therapy? Which has the potential to cause most damage — drugs or vitamins?

The chief problem with gaining acceptance for vitamin therapy is that there's no 'scientific evidence' that it works. There is no scientific evidence that it does not work either! My cynical husband believes that the onus should be on the anti-vitamin people to produce evidence that vitamins don't work. When you think of it, he has a point.

Obtaining scientific evidence on vitamins is almost a lost cause. Even Dr Pauling said in 1989 that because of lack of funds, he was experiencing severe difficulties continuing with research. No company can claim ownership of a vitamin, so I guess there is little incentive to finance research. A patent can be taken out on a drug, but a vitamin is simply an organic compound.

How then can the authorities consider making vitamins available only on prescription?

What happened to the 'placebo effect'? It seems even more farcical when we consider that anti-histamine tablets and salbutamol puffers can be purchased over the counter without prescription. These products have CAUTION S3 written boldly on them, indicating they have been listed on the Poisons Register. In 1987 no poison warning had yet appeared on a vitamin bottle, but some vested interests seem to be suggesting we should require a prescription for vitamins!

Do you smell a rat?

DANNY'S ASTHMA ATTACK

After eight extremely healthy years, we had our confidence shattered.

Danny suffered a severe attack of asthma. Twice in the one day I was forced to take him to the doctor to be attached to the machine we abhorred. As a mother, I felt strange helping a six foot, twenty-one year old in and out of the doctor's surgery. Danny didn't take it too well either, seeming to regard the whole episode as an insult! On both occasions, when we arrived home, he fell into a strange type of sleep; his whole body trembled. This experience upset me considerably; not the least disturbing aspect being the cost of his medication. (Danny was still at university and dependent on us at the time.)

I remembered the woman who said 'Asthma means poverty to me...' How do they cope with the cost of medication?

Danny recovered completely in three days, but I developed what was probably the same virus. I didn't suffer the constant asthma that afflicted Danny; mine was breathing difficulties during the night.

The first thing I did was increase the vitamin A, but to no avail. I doubled the dose; still no improvement. Increasing the vitamin E had no effect. Next I tried changing brands — still no difference. Something was wrong.

Devastated, I was convinced the vitamins had let me down. I was forced to take Theodur® nightly and, although it was more effective than the Nuelin®, it still caused side-effects, e.g. shakiness in the legs, hyperactivity and slight nausea. Although these effects lessened as the days passed, I was worried.

In a newspaper article, Lady Phyllis Cilento claimed the only effective treatment against viral infection, was vitamin C. As I was convinced I had a virus, I followed the good doctor's advice, and added one teaspoon of vitamin C powder (Calcium Ascorbate) to my usual vitamins. I took the vitamin C as one would a course of antibiotics, e.g. one teaspoon three times a day for five days. (In retrospect, it seems a high dose of vitamin C but as diarrhoea didn't develop, I mustn't have overdone it.)

Within twenty-four hours I no longer required the Theodur® and had saved myself from resorting to stronger medication. To this day I still take a half teaspoon of vitamin C powder per day.

I wrote to the asthmatics who had maintained contact (who were taking the vitamins) and explained why I had added vitamin C to my regime.

Around this time (1987) Queensland was dubbed the 'Asthma Capital of the World.' Dr Charles Mitchell in a survey of 3,438 Queensland children found that Murarrie, Ferny Grove, Gladstone and Bundaberg were among the worst areas for asthma. The incidence of the disease in children was 50 per cent higher in Queensland than in Tasmania. The Asthma Foundation reported that the death rate from asthma had more than doubled. In 1975 approx. 2 per 100,000 people died, in 1985 it had reached 5 per 100,000.

The Emeritus Consultant Physician at the Royal Adelaide Hospital, Dr Munro-Ford said:

'These are grim figures indeed when one considers the multitude of new drugs now available, the increased awareness and patient understanding about their disease and the existence of active, well-endowed asthma foundations in every State.'

There was a time when asthma was not considered fatal. What has changed?

It can be neither natural nor co-incidental for this deterioration to occur in the health of a nation. What is wrong?

If you are over forty-five, can you recall any asthma sufferers at your school?

Today's children know at least five or six in their class alone who are asthmatic!

Why?

THE PROBLEM WITH GUINEA-PIGS

At forty-five years of age, I was besieged with problems again, caused chiefly I believe, by that incurable disease — AGE.

When we reach forty-five, our bodies undergo changes. One of these is the necessity to wear reading glasses. Almost every woman I knew was having to rummage in her handbag to read a restaurant menu. On a few hilarious occasions, only one in our group remembered her spectacles and when the menu arrived, that one pair had to be passed around the entire table.

Maybe there was a connection between all those women needing spectacles and the body's ability to absorb vitamin A? I should have realised that the quantity of vitamins sufficient for a thirty-eight year old, would not meet the requirements for a forty-five year old. As the body ages, it tends to lose some of its ability to absorb nutrients, and as the gift of sight is very closely associated with vitamin A, I wondered about this.

Why didn't I consider all this when asthma struck once more?

This time, it wasn't only disturbed nights; this was the real thing.

During a family outing at Sanctuary Cove (a then new resort near the Gold Coast) I experienced the disabling effects of asthma. It was a beautiful autumn day, crisp and sunny, the sea and sky shimmering. One could not imagine ill-health when surrounded by such clear air.

We decided to wander along the boardwalk overlooking the yacht harbour. That's when it hit me. Even to walk the short distance, from one side of the boardwalk to the other, was beyond me!

Because the asthma of the previous year appeared to be viral related, I assumed the same of this new outbreak. Therefore, I increased the vitamin C to three teaspoons per day — no improvement whatsoever; doubling the vitamin A to 40,000 units and increasing the E to 500 mg produced no results either. This time I believed I was truly beaten.

Another day during this distressing period remains in my memory, primarily because it illustrates the anguish suffered by very severe asthmatics.

We had promised the twins some guinea-pigs for their birthday; (must have had rocks in our heads). We sallied forth to the pet shop which had a long cement ramp from the footpath to the door. Normally I'd have bounded up such a ramp, but on this day, the struggle to negotiate that incline was enormous. I suddenly believed I could see the future. I knew, should this condition remain, I would be lucky to last another decade. 'How long,' I wondered, 'could a heart sustain this effort?' Deep sadness prompted the additional thought, 'Life would scarcely be worth living anyway.'

For ten days, (while taking Theodur® at night) I experimented with the vitamins, attempting to find the correct ratio. The future looked bleak as I could see no alternative to either constant use of a puffer, cortisone, or probably both.

Before ringing the doctor, I decided to make one last attempt with the vitamins. In her book *Medical Mother*, Lady Cilento set out a vitamin regime for the treatment of chronic respiratory tract infections. She mentioned that asthma would benefit from this regime.

In the past I regarded her recommendation of 60,000 units of vitamin A as completely 'over the top'. However, I was desperate. Surely no harm would befall a person taking larger amounts for only a few days?

In the good Australian tradition, I 'gave it a go' and took six 10,000 unit capsules per day. Within two days of commencing this larger dose, I felt marvellous. Even though I stayed on the high dosage for three months, I suffered no side-effects. By the beginning of June I was in fine spirits, and the remainder of the year included some freezing, but magical days and nights at Expo 88.

I couldn't help thinking of Mrs. Leone Edwards, who died of an asthma attack shortly before the opening of Expo. Ironically, her husband Sir Llew Edwards, was the driving force behind this international exhibition where millions enjoyed themselves.

I wrote to the other asthma sufferers, and told them of my new dosage, and included the following table:

AT AGE 45

Min. Temp.	Vitamin Dose
4• to 8 •(celc)	60,000 i.u. A, 500 mg E, 3 teasp. C.
8• to 15•	30,000 i.u. A, 500 mg E, 1 teasp. C.
15• and over	20,000 i.u. A, 500 mg E, ½ teasp. C.
Very hot days	Omit altogether unless you react to high humidity.

Lady Cilento wrote:

> 'Large doses, 60,000 to 90,000 units, are sometimes
>
> needed for chronic respiratory infections. These doses are non-toxic when taken with Vitamin E and C and not continued for more than three months; then reduce dose to 40,000, but do not cease.'

Not being a chronic respiratory infection sufferer, I sometimes omit vitamins during hot weather. This seems to me a good idea, just in case I did accumulate too much during winter.

When the weather turned cool, I re-commenced the higher doses and this enabled me to play squash throughout the year with not so much as a wheeze.

VITAMIN A — THE KING OF VITAMINS

It is not easy to obtain sufficient daily intake of this vitamin from our usual Australian diet.

VITAMIN A FOODS

Listed below is a chart containing various foods and their accompanying vitamin A levels: (from *Clinical Dietetics and Nutrition*).

You will note: *'Only one third of beta carotene is absorbed and only one half of what is absorbed is converted to vitamin A. Thus <u>only one sixth</u> of dietary beta carotene is converted to vitamin A.'*

VITAMIN A OR CAROTENE CONTENT OF VARIOUS FOODS

Food	Vitamin A i.u. per 100gram	Food	*Carotene i.u.per 100gram
Halibut-liver oil	4,000,000	Carrots-mature	20,000
Cod-liver oil	200,000	Spinach	13,000
Liver, sheep	45,000	Beet leaves	11,000
Liver, ox	15,000	Carrots, young	10,000
Liver, pig	5,000	Cress	8,000
Liver, calf	4,000	Kale	8,000
Butter	3,500	Sweet potato	6,000
Cheese		Watercress	5,000
(whole fat)	1,500	Apricot	2.000
Eggs, hen	1,100	Lettuce	2,000
Kidney, ox	1,000	Tomato	1.200
Salmon, canned	250	Peach	800
Milk, summer	150	Brussels sprouts	700
Herrings, fresh	100	Cabbage	500
Milk, winter	75	Maize, yellow	350
Beef or mutton	20		

Divide by 6

The second column in the above chart, mentions the top carotene containing foods and gives the amount of units contained in 100 grams. As carotene has to be converted into vitamin A within the body, the actual amount extracted from the carotene would be much lower than indicated.

Therefore in order to ascertain the quantity of vitamin A received from each fruit and vegetable, **we are required to divide the figures in the right hand column, by six.**

Carotene is converted into vitamin A primarily in the <u>intestinal wall</u>.

PLEASE NOTE: Diabetics are incapable of converting carotene into vitamin A. (*Clinical Dietetics and Nutrition*).

As we can see, unless we take cod or halibut-liver oil or eat some type of liver at least once a week, our diet would probably not supply the 1988 Recommended Daily Allowance of 5,000 units of vitamin A.

Why then are we continually being told vitamin supplements are not necessary?

Michael B. Sporn, M.D. of the American National Cancer Institute, believes we should be concerned about consuming too little vitamin A. He claims there is a definite connection between cancer rates and low levels of vitamin A. I quote his statement from *The Complete Book of Vitamins*:

> *'The data at hand clearly indicates that any human population at risk of cancer, should not be allowed to remain in a vitamin A deficient state.'*

Are we at risk of cancer?

Do you recall Dr Linus Pauling, the

double Nobel Prize winner? He argued <u>against</u> a move in America to restrict vitamin A capsules to 10,000 units.

A further quote from the publication *Improving your Health with Vitamin A* p. 69, indicates how the body uses natural vitamin A: 'Whatever you don't need on a daily basis is stored in your liver.'

Children need much less vitamin A than adults. Lady Cilento suggests cod liver oil as a source of vitamin A for children — 1 teaspoon to 1 tablespoon a day according to age. (Surely she meant Hypol®, Scott's Emulsion® or cod-liver oil capsules!) In her book *Medical Mother* p.87, she suggests the Vitamin E dose for children should be 50 mg to 100 mg.

Lady Cilento also included a paragraph on vitamin A overdose in her book *Vitamin and Mineral Deficiencies*:

'Too much vitamin A can be toxic, causing thinning hair, sore lips, bruising, nose bleeds, headaches, blurred vision, flaky itching skin, painful joints and bones. But for toxicity to occur, you would have to take over 100,000 units a day for a long time. These symptoms can be prevented by generous doses of vitamin C — say 1000 mg a day — but even if vitamin C and E are not taken, the symptoms com-pletely disappear in a few days after ceasing vitamin A'.

A chart of over-dose symptoms distributed by **Bio-Concepts**, Kelvin Grove, Qld., states that an acute toxic dose would be 250,000 units per day. A chronic overdose would be 60,000 to 90,000 units per day for six months, so they are more conservative than Lady Cilento.

To emphasise individual reactions to dosages: a Brisbane nutritionist told me that she suffers symptoms on only 30,000 units, yet I take 60,000 for more than three months with no side-effects.

It bears reiterating that there must be wide variations in each person's daily requirement for this vitamin, and we must also keep in mind that any <u>overdose is reversible within a few days of ceasing the vitamin.</u>

The American Recommended Daily Allowance for Vitamin A (1980) is alarmingly low, particularly when we consider Dr Sporn's assertion on the relation between cancer rates and vitamin A deficiency.

They recommend 5,000 units for a boy of 11 and a man over 51, regardless of the difference in age, body-weight, exercise levels, stress levels and general state of health.

Remember this: 5,000 does not just represent the level of vitamin A received from supplements, it includes the total amount of vitamin A received in the daily food as well.

At least (in 1980,) the American Daily allowance recognises that pregnant and lactating women require more vitamin A than others. They add another 1,000 units for pregnancy and an extra 2,000 units for breast-feeding to the female recommendation of 4,000 units. ('Foundations of Normal and Therapeutic Nutrition').

Not only do vitamin needs vary from individual to individual but some people, like my husband, are perfectly healthy without the help of <u>any</u> vitamin supplements whatsoever while I require, during winter, at least 40,000 units <u>per day.</u>

In her book *Vitamins and your Health*, nutritionist Ann Gildroy claims that,in the time of scurvy, although the sailers were eating identical foods, many succumbed to the disease and died, while others remained unscathed. Food for thought?

The founder of Vitamin Therapy, Dr Abram Hoffer, helps illustrate this point. In 1951, Dr Hoffer gave large amounts of vitamin B3 to hallucinating patients, even though they were not suffering from the vitamin B3 deficiency disease, pellagra. They recovered from their psychosis. He believes they simply had a much larger than usual requirement for this vitamin. (From *Dr Atkins' Nutrition Breakthrough*).

Dr Hoffer's experiment was the forerunner of Orthomolecular Medicine. Dr Linus Pauling coined the term 'orthomolecular' which means the importance of making the biochemical environment just right.

Frankly, I believe we should ignore most of the Recommended Daily Requirements. The American, Dr. Irwin Stone, obviously agrees:

> *'The Food and Nutrition Board has been reducing the RDA for ascorbate (Vit. C) with each new edition of their book 'Recommended Dietary Allowances'. In 1958, the adult RDA for ascorbate was 75 mg, in 1968 it went down to 60 mg, and in their latest exploit in 1975, it lost another 25% and became 35 mg. If the Food and Nutrition Board continues whittling away at its present rate, the RDA (for Vit.C) will be zero by the year 2,000.'*
>
> *(The Complete Book Of Vitamins)*

The vitamin A chart recommends liver as a good source of vitamin A. This chart omits the tropical fruit, paw-paw, which is very rich in carotene and delicious with lemon juice and sugar — much more appetising than liver; yuk! While liver does contain large amounts of A, it also has a tendency to collect high levels of pesticides and other poisons.

I quote from *Toxicology of Pesticides*:

'Partly because of their great importance for bio-transformation and excretion, the liver and kidneys often show high concentrations of foreign chemicals.'

I wonder if it's wise to consume large amounts of liver, if, as also mentioned in this publication:

'DDT is found in virtually everyone in the general population of USA and other countries'.

We can be sure beasts are also affected, although lamb's fry, being from a young animal, should be the safest.

Every one, from the sailor in bygone ages to the asthmatic of today, is different, and we all require varying amounts of nutrients. Some seem to need large amounts of vitamin A to remain healthy, while others probably risk overdose by 'looking' at a paw-paw!

My advice is — listen to your body.

It doesn't know its supposed daily requirements — it only knows what it <u>needs</u>.

SPECULATIONS ON CHILDHOOD HEALTH

In 1989, Australia was visited by an American, Dr Berger. His controversial theories were aired on both television and radio. I heard the word 'asthma' on a radio talk-back program and paused to listen. Dr Berger claimed that milk was the chief cause of asthma and most asthmatics would be cured if they eliminated dairy products from their diets, cut back on allergy causing foods and added extra vitamins.

When I heard this, I thought, 'What a load of tripe!' Past generations of Australians had eaten dairy products constantly, and yet appeared to suffer very little asthma.

A nutritionist from Sydney University, Ms Jenny O'Dea, stated that thirty years ago, Australian children drank twice the amount of milk that they drink today — (*The Courier Mail* 27/4/91).

Conversely, Denmark is one of the few countries where the incidence of asthma has not increased, yet it is famous for its dairy produce. (*Breathing Space* magazine Jan. 1987).

Don't get me wrong, I believe a person can be allergic to milk. We can be allergic to practically anything. I simply can't accept that every asthmatic is allergic to milk.

I decided to ring the talk-back host and give my opinion. My knees were wobbling but I said to myself, 'Marian, don't be such a coward. Get on that phone and tell them straight!' So I did.

I told him that I would suggest asthmatics try vitamins first before giving up dairy foods. The host surprised me with his question: 'Do you eat dairy products?'

'Yes,' I replied.

'Why are you still eating dairy products?'

I felt like a criminal in the dock, but mastered my nerves sufficiently to answer

'Because I don't believe it makes any difference.' I went on to tell him about the vitamin treatment.

'Vitamin A,' he said, 'isn't that one of those vitamins that accumulates in the body?'

'Yes. But I take it chiefly in the winter and only a little in summer. I believe that any accumulation is used up in summer.'

He accepted that.

Those statistics on milk, as quoted by Ms O'Dea, caused me to wonder whether somewhere along the line we haven't lost the plot for rearing healthy children. As I said earlier, our low levels of vitamin A could be attributed to pesticides, preservatives or some other chemical in the body. However, there is another aspect which would have exacerbated this problem.

During the 1940s and 1950s, children were routinely given doses of cod-liver oil (an excellent source of vitamin A and D). I can recall sitting on the kitchen table with my small brother, while our mother dispensed huge spoonfuls of Scott's Emulsion®. At boarding school after the war, my husband and his brother were called to the nurse's office every night to receive their dose of cod-liver oil. (Both my husband and I were very thin children.)

Following a holiday period from my boarding school, practically every girl in our dormitory arrived back with a bottle of cod-liver oil capsules. We had all contracted severe chest infections during the preceding winter and these girls, who were aged fifteen or sixteen, must have been recommended these by their doctors or chemists.

I wonder if the parents and doctors of that time were concerned about T.B.? Perhaps they believed that thin children, or those suffering chronic chest problems, might be candidates for tuberculosis. Perhaps all that cod-liver oil not only protected us against T.B., but prevented asthma.

This medical interest in the nutritional approach to respiratory diseases, seemed to have dissipated by the 1960s. The advent of antibiotics could have contributed to this.

When I told a doctor that our eldest child, then aged three, seemed to experience fewer chest infections while taking Hypol® (a cod-liver oil mixture) he scarcely bothered to answer. He simply proceeded to write a prescription for more antibiotics. On another occasion I told a doctor that this same child seemed to suffer no tonsillitis when we had plenty of oranges in the house. He dismissed me with a snort, and said 'What are you, a nurse or something?'.

Is it any wonder mothers lose faith in the medical profession?

Danny, our eldest, suffered chest infections, ear infections, tonsillitis and eventually bronchial asthma by the time he was three. He also underwent two operations; all before his fourth birthday.

Our other five children rarely saw the inside of a doctor's surgery.

There could be a simple explanation for this. The good health of our other children could have been due to plain good luck. I sometimes wonder, however, whether the reason our eldest had so many problems was because I knew so little about vitamins or minerals when he was born.

I was going to be the perfect mother.

None of that powdered formula stuff for me! Immediately following an enforced weaning at two months, I put Danny straight on to fresh cow's milk. None of that red cordial-looking Rose Hip Syrup either! My baby would have freshly squeezed orange juice.

It wasn't until my second child arrived, and not doing at all well on this diet, that I realised I could have been on the wrong track.

My general practitioner in Rockhampton (who was ahead of his time, I'm sure) told me there was very little iron in cow's milk and if I wished to persist with it, I'd have to add extra iron drops to each feeding bottle. As I was already adding Pentavite® drops, this extra chore made milk preparation positively tedious.

I took the easy way out and established this child and all who followed, on powdered infant formulas. These formulae all contained added vitamins and minerals.

It was also pointed out to me, that fresh orange juice can sometimes be stale orange juice, and that oranges, in fact, contain less vitamin C than the previously disdained Rose Hip Syrup.

As the children grew older, I always kept a bottle of vitamin C on hand and issued tablets to anyone with a sniffle. I also believe the vitamin A capsules I took throughout my final pregnancy contributed to the twins' strong resistance to infection.

Whatever the reason, the fact remains that during early childhood our eldest seemed to be forever on antibiotics or in hospital, while our five other children suffered few illnesses. Frankly, I don't believe these things happen accidentally.

POLAR BEAR LIVER AND GRAPE OVERDOSE

It was exceptionally cold in Brisbane in 1990. Temperatures of one degree were recorded. As previously mentioned, cold weather triggers my asthma. Each day, I 'insured' against attacks by taking vitamins A,E and C to their limit (e.g. 60,000 units vit.A, 500 mg vit.E, 3 teasp. vit.C powder). On a couple of <u>extremely</u> cold days asthma forced me to increase the A to 80,000 units. Notwithstanding, it was a very successful year, asthma-wise.

There was one major incident, however, which I'm ashamed to admit.

How many times had I heard the medical opinion regarding vitamin A and the dangers of overdose? So many times the following had been related to me: 'A group of explorers went to the Arctic where they ate nothing but polar-bear liver. These men subsequently died because polar bear liver is extremely high in vitamin A.'

On first hearing the polar bear story, I had difficulty maintaining a straight face. (First, catch your bear...) We'd recently arrived home from a holiday in Sydney, where we'd searched Taronga Park Zoo and failed to find even one polar bear — maybe they'd eaten too many 'toxic' explorers.

This is not to say that too much vitamin A is not harmful. It certainly is, but then practically anything in overdose is harmful, even water. (Three deaths from water overdose were recorded by psychiatrists at the University of British Columbia.) A common English description for vitamin A overdose, is 'vitamin A intoxication'. A 'hangover' would be a more accurate description than 'intoxication'.

As implied earlier, during that winter in 1990, I accidentally overdosed on vitamin A.

Looking back, I can't believe I did it. For some reason (probably economical) I bought some liquid vitamin A.

Somehow, after reading the instructions on the bottle, I believed that to obtain 10,000 units I had to fill the dropper completely instead of only to the indicating line.

This monumental mistake meant a dose of three to four times my usual cold weather amount, and the multiplication would have equalled approximately 250,000 units per day.

Why didn't I know something was wrong? Even when the drops were added to fruit juice, the taste was worse than dreadful. I knew I couldn't continue for long.

On the first night, I went to bed with a severe headache and took two aspirin — got that dose right. The second night, the same thing. The third night, ditto. I'm one of those lucky people who almost never suffers headaches, so I knew something was wrong. At 2.00am the next day, the penny dropped. I remembered a wise woman's warning: 'You'll know if you ever overdose. The symptom is a severe headache.'

I jumped out of bed: the temperature was a freezing two degrees ('freezing' to Queenslanders anyway) and ran into the kitchen to re-read the label on the bottle. Sure enough I'd overdosed. No wonder my head was thumping. Within a day of ceasing all vitamin A, the headache disappeared.

I took no vitamins at all for the following week to allow my system to use up the excess. Neither my asthma nor general health suffered any ill effects from this overdose, although ever since that episode I can't bear the thought of liquid vitamin A.

It's not easy to overdose — but it can be done!

Looking back on my overdose, I shouldn't take all the responsibility. Perhaps, I'm looking for an excuse but the instructions on the label were in very small print, and not very clear anyway. If I could make a mistake, surely others could do the same. Even when I understood the directions, the hand-eye co-ordination required to fill that darn dropper 'exactly to the line', was beyond me.

It is not logical to label any substance 'dangerous' or 'poisonous' simply because it's possible to overdose on it. If this were so, all the following substances would have to be labelled 'POISON': tea, coffee, wine, spirits, aspirin etc, and as I said previously, even water.

Let me tell you an amusing tale which illustrates the absurdity of horror stories.

Did you realise there are few things more dangerous, in overdose, than the humble grape? Grapes should be sold with warnings attached; telling of the dire consequences of overdosing on this seemingly harmless and healthy fruit.

This is experience talking. Many years ago, my brother and I fell victim to this dangerous fruit. I was eight and he was ten and we were taken to a farm in Central Queensland known locally as 'The Oasis'. It truly deserved the name.

This part of Queensland is hot and dry, yet this farmer had transformed his land into a luxuriant display of exotic fruits. Grapes were his favourite and he grew every variety imaginable. They were delicious.

We were given a bucket and told we could collect and eat as many grapes as we liked. We thought we were in heaven.

The following day we couldn't go to school because we spent the entire twelve hours writhing in agonising pain. I had never been so sick; and I wonder why doctors don't warn us about this dangerous fruit.

Practically every 'good thing' can be overdone to the point where it becomes a 'bad thing'.

It is my conviction that no-one,

particularly asthmatics, should deny themselves adequate doses of vitamin A simply because it's possible to overdose.

Actually after my experience with vitamin A overdose, I'm amazed that anyone could continue long enough to arrive at the hair-loss and flaky-skin stage. The headaches would force most people to quit.

Some doctors persist in attacking vitamins A and E. Newspaper articles still appear from time to time showing bias against these vitamins, yet you don't often read about the dangers inherent in overdosing on *other* vitamins and minerals. My nutritionist claims it is possible to experience over-dose symptoms on practically all of them. As Lady Cilento said 'the symptoms completely disappear in a few days after ceasing vitamin A'. (*Vitamin and Mineral Deficiencies* p.9.)

Why all the fuss?

REFLECTIONS

As previously stated, vitamin E is an essential ingredient in this treatment and ascertaining the correct amount of E is important. In 1983, I saw some Accomin® Multi Vitamin Capsules, and noticed they contained 10,000 units of vitamin A, and 5 units of vitamin E. I decided they might be preferable to separate A and E capsules. Wrong! My chest tightened within two days of commencing them. Evidently <u>a good does of Vitamin E</u> is required to make the treatment effective.

<u>While on 10,000 units of vitamin A, I</u>

<u>found 100 mg of synthetic E was the minimum
amount required to obtain results.</u>

This brings me to the subject of synthetic
E. As I said earlier, during the early 1980s
synthetic E was practically the only type
available. I found it extremely effective, so
long as it didn't contain wheat germ oil (I'm
allergic to wheat germ oil — it causes
abdominal distress).

I still prefer synthetic E on the advice of a
chemist who told me it is more stable.
However it is becoming very difficult to find
any without wheat germ oil.

Recently, extra information on natural
vitamin E has caused me to reconsider. Now I
buy natural vitamin E direct from the
distributor. It has been successful, which no
doubt means their product is fresh. The reason
I rejected it in the first place was because it
simply didn't work. However, I quote Dr M.
Colgan's opinion on natural vitamin E:

*'Buy it fresh. Vitamin E starts to oxidise in the
capsules within a few months of manufacture.'*

Dr Colgan also states:

*'This is the one case where a natural vitamin is
better than the synthetic.'*

from (*Your Personal Vitamin Profile* p. 147).

In the past, I may have bought stale natural vitamin E and that could have rendered it ineffective.

Another point which Lady Cilento stressed when speaking of fat soluble vitamins, is that they should be consumed with a meal containing a little fat or oil to call forth bile for their digestion.

As for the timing of vitamin doses, experience has taught me the most important dose of the day is at breakfast. Lunch and tea-time doses can be late, but in very cold weather, my 'preventative' breakfast dose must be taken <u>before</u> 9a.m.

The reason this first dose is important is that all my severe asthma attacks occurred at 3.OO or 4.00am. Research on rats has shown that vitamin A causes a 'beneficial compound to be formed in the lungs within eighteen hours. (*Improving Your Health with Vitamin A* p.15). I have also found through experience that there is about a twenty-hour time lapse before vitamin A begins to work. Therefore I have to ensure that the breakfast dose is taken so I will be protected in the early hours of the morning. To maintain good health, this timing is crucial for me during periods of infection or very cold weather.

Which brings me to another aspect of weather conditions. It is necessary to be conscious of uncharacteristic changes in temperatures. Should the climate suddenly cool during the warmer months, vitamin A has to be increased — and <u>quickly</u>. Similarly a warm period during winter months, calls for a reduction in dose.

An example of a sudden drop in temperature happened in the winter of 1991 when I had to increase my vitamin A intake to 120,000 units for the short period of a week. (Don't faint I'm still alive and kicking.) The cold weather brought with it asthma.

Only large doses of A would control it. The remainder of winter was extremely mild and 40,000 units per day was sufficient.

You will probably consider 120,000 units a ridiculous amount of vitamin A, even for such a short period, but I need to prove that vitamin therapy is the complete answer, so I try to avoid all drugs. I would also ask you to remember that hormonal changes can exacerbate asthma. In the past I controlled it beautifully, for seven years, on very low doses of vitamin A. It is also worth remembering that (during those seven years) my son Danny and I required no medication, no special diet, no exercises, no meditation and very little faith — only the vitamins.

My advice to anyone harbouring doubts

about vitamin treatment is simply this: 'Try it yourself for one week only and see how you feel.'

I'm convinced there is some psychological aspect to achieving the correct dose. I always get to the point where I don't want to increase the A, but when I remember the original premise Asthma is a Vitamin A Deficiency and I listen to my body's signals, I can happily take that little bit extra to make the symptoms disappear.

When we consider that, in times of crises, the amount of Ventolin® (administered by nebuliser) is multiplied by fifty and in some cases to the unbelievable amount of one hundred times, it is understandable why sufferers using only vitamins will sometimes need to substantially increase their usual dose. I have found during times of infections, etcetera it helps to abandon all fears of overdosing. Let's face it, vitamins can't possibly cause the over-dosing problems related to drugs, and what alternative is there? (To my mind, cortisone is <u>not</u> a viable alternative.)

These days I find myself saying, 'If I need it — I'll take it. If I don't — I won't.'

This table sets out my vitamin dosages over the years.

Age	Summer	Winter
38	Nil to 10,000 units Vit.A, 100 mg syn.E	10,000 to 20,000 i.u. Vit.A, 100 mg Vit.E
43	10,000 i.u. Vit.A, 200 mg syn. Vit.E	30,000 i.u. Vit.A 400 mg syn. Vit.E

Also started to add vitamin C powder for viruses.

Age	Summer	Winter
45-51	10,000 - 20.000 units Vit. A, 200 mg syn.E	60,000 units Vit.A, 500 mg syn.E 3 teasp. Vit.C powder per day (if necessary).
53	10,000 - 20,000 i.u. Vit.A, 500 i.u. natural Vit.E.	10,000 to 40,000 i.u. Vit.A, 500 i.u. natural Vit.E, 1 teasp. Vit.C powder (Calc. Ascorbate)

Since turning 53, my requirements for vitamin A has dropped considerably. I'm not sure why — perhaps it is age-related.

MEDICAL BIAS

Medical bias could be justified. We've all met the fanatic who believes that every illness known to mankind can be cured with a plethora of vitamins — and very expensive ones at that. Still this doesn't excuse those whose bias against any form of vitamin supplementation is so transparent as to be almost comical. Take the following two examples; one from a radio program and the other, a local newspaper:

First, a conversation in February, 1991, between a radio interviewer and a paediatrician.

<u>Interviewer</u>: 'Are children these days being given too much medication?'

<u>Doctor</u>: 'Oh! definitely. You get these over-anxious mothers who are forever popping vitamins into the kids' mouths, so when they get older they will turn to pills or other substances, like alcohol and tobacco, to make them feel better.'

Stunned silence from interviewer.

Note: Interviewer used the word 'medication'. Doctor said 'vitamins'.

The second example concerns an article published in *The Sunday Mail* on 21st July, 1991, headlined:

'Doctors Angry over Pill-popping Habits.'

The article began by stating the medical profession was 'greatly annoyed' by the sporting world's use of vitamins and minerals to enhance performance. The article went on to claim 'doctors say the pill-popping habit exacts a devastating price.' It then proceeded to link vitamin and mineral use with illegal steroid dosing. The tragic case of an American footballer dying of brain cancer, attributed to steroids, was then outlined. The insinuation was such that the reader was left associating brain cancer with vitamins and minerals.

The obvious bias in this report would be apparent to most readers. However, there is always the concern that some might take the article at face value.

The above examples give us an insight into the opposition many patients encounter when they ask their doctor for a more natural treatment.

Is the best argument in favour of vitamins the medical profession's opposition to them? Do we fight something we do not fear? Does anyone believe the anti-vitamin brigade is simply protecting us from ourselves?

Could the medical hip-pocket nerve be involved?

Many doctors are justifiably admired for their honesty, dedication and hard work. Their profession must be the most rewarding, yet the most difficult of all careers. We can only guess at the trauma and heartache they must witness and endure.

It is very sad, then, to encounter one who is in the profession simply for the money. I met a young man in a doctor's waiting room who told me he was at university studying medicine. 'What made you decide to become a doctor?' I asked.

'I went for a drive around and found that the biggest houses, with the biggest cars and boats out the front, all belonged to doctors so I thought " That's the life for me!".'

Let us hope he now works in research and wasn't let loose on the public.

Today, the attitude prevails that if you have the academic ability to achieve the top Tertiary Entrance Score, you will automatically study medicine — Why? Is it because society presumes medicine is the ultimate earner? Our second eldest, who achieved this score, was amazed at the number of people who assumed he would choose medicine.

Ideally, the medical profession should be regarded as a vocation — not a business. Doctors deal with lives, not motor-cars. No one should become very wealthy from the bad luck, pain and misery of others. Besides, should a mechanic fail to fix our car, we can refuse to pay him; not so the doctor should he fail to fix our body.

It seems then, that if some doctors perceive themselves as businessmen, then, to protect our interest, we may be forced to consider ourselves 'clients' or 'customers'.

The word 'patient' is defined in the Concise Oxford Dictionary thus:

> _Patient_ adj.& n. - adj. having or showing _patience_ - n.a. person receiving or registered to receive medical treatment.

Patience n. 1. *Calm endurance of hardship, provocation, pain, delay, etc. 2. tolerant perseverance or forbearance. 3. the capacity for calm self-possessed waiting ...*

This connotation, to me, spells v-i-c-t-i-m.

DOSAGE AND DEFICIENCY DILEMMA

In order to keep bronchitis at bay while pregnant with the twins, I took an occasional 5,000 unit capsule of vitamin A. Recently however, there has been much controversy about pregnancy and vitamin A.

In 1991, I found a book (Antia F.P. *Clinical Dietetics and Nutrition* Bombay; Oxford University Press 1989) which stated that doses exceeding 10,000 units of vitamin A per day, should <u>not</u> be given to pregnant women <u>who are suffering vitamin A deficiencies.</u>

10,000 units seems conservative when we

consider that a woman eating one liver meal could ingest approx. 50,000 units of vitamin A.

Our tall, slender twins were (and still are) extremely healthy people, yet on a recent purchase of vitamin A tablets (5,000 units), I found the following:

> 'WARNING: *Taking more than half a tablet per day during pregnancy may cause birth defects.'*

Ridiculous! Half a tablet would equal 2,500 units.

Absolutely stunned, I rang the vitamin company to make inquiries. I was told that government regulations in July, 1993 dictated that vitamin A must be sold with the above warning. The reason for the restriction was the reported foetal abnormalities produced by mothers ingesting 250,000 units of vitamin A per day.

Surely nobody could take 250,000 units for longer than a few days. Remember this was the toxic dose I accidentally took for three days. How could these women tolerate the headaches?

I've recently spoken to a few Health Department officials about this regulation and each time a different amount of vitamin A has been mentioned regarding the overdosing mothers. I've tried to get more information from Canberra but so far nothing has arrived.

A vitamin company representative said the regulation was an over-kill. What an understatement!

The Medical Journal of Australia Vol. 157, states that a South Australian report estimated the daily intake of vitamin A in that state to be 5,000 units. United States surveys show considerably higher averages of 7,000 - 8,000 i.u. per day.

Theoretically if 'more than 2,500 units per day may cause birth defects', South Australia and the United States of America should have very high incidences of birth defects, which of course is nonsense.

Pregnant women who suffer asthma must feel they are in a no-win situation. They are warned off vitamin A in doses higher than half a tablet, and medical information from MIMS shows that the following drugs are not recommended during pregnancy:

> *VENTOLIN®: Not to be used in pregnancy or if wanting to become pregnant. Drug passes over to baby. Not recommended for breastfeeding mothers.*

> *ORAL CORTICOSTEROIDS: In animal tests, these drugs produce abortion, cleft palate and skeletal malformations. Could reduce the*

performance of the adrenal glands in babies.
Breastfeeding: Appears in breast-milk and
could suppress growth of baby or reduce func-
tions of adrenal glands.

POISON S4

NUELIN®: Appears in breast milk so doses
must be kept low to avoid toxicity to baby.

If doctors are concerned that too much
vitamin A harms the foetus, shouldn't they
also be concerned about medication
transferring to the baby?

Where are the WARNINGS on Cortisone,
Ventolin® or Nuelin® labels?

Is the government relying on doctors to
warn women? Can all doctors remember to
warn <u>every</u> woman of child-bearing age of the
dangers of cortisone and other drugs?

Do they ask if she is breast-feeding?
Would they know she is <u>thinking</u> of becoming
pregnant? The warnings should be clearly
printed on the labels.

The same nutrition book which espouses
conservative doses of vitamin A in pregnancy,
goes on to state that where severe deficiencies
are common, such as in India, women are
given a dose of 200,000 units of vitamin A
immediately following delivery of their babies.

This is to build up the A in the mother's milk supply. Evidently milk must not deliver too much vitamin A to the baby.

There certainly seems to be confusion regarding pregnancy and vitamin A. Doctor Antia writes that numerous babies and children in India suffer blindness because of vitamin A deficiencies (even well-off children) yet, in Australia, doctors warn pregnant women off vitamin A completely.

Lady Cilento claimed foetal abnormalities are caused by a lack of vitamin A and the book *Biochemical Basis of Medicine* 1985, backs up her claim with a list of nine symptoms of vitamin A deficiency.

A precis of that list includes the following symptoms: Inability to see in the dark; failure of growth; dryness of mucus membranes of lungs, digestive tract, urinary tract and secondary infection; faulty bone modelling; nerve lesions; abnormal enlargement of the head; <u>degeneration of testes and abortion or production of malformed offspring</u>; certain forms of skin disease; death (resulting from serious deficiency).

The book then proceeds to list six symptoms of vitamin A overdose: Failure of growth (rats); skin abnormalities (rat and man); increased pressure in skull (infant);

vomiting (man); bone abnormalities (man); fatal internal haemorrhage (rat); birth malformations (rat).

An interesting point here is that these overdose symptoms are similar to the deficiency symptoms.

Is this indicating that a pregnant woman with too little vitamin A in her system risks miscarriage or malformed offspring and one who is overdosing runs the same risk?

Personally, I would be much more concerned about too little vitamin A than too much. Australians on the whole would be more likely to be deficient in this vitamin. Lady Cilento said that from her observations of ordinary diets, she found many to be 'woefully deficient' in vitamin A. (*Medical Mother* p.86).

Let us consider an average nourishing Australian meal consisting of roast chicken, white potatoes, corn on the cob and cabbage followed by a plate of fresh peaches and ice-cream (not homemade). First class meal, we would say, but that meal would deliver only a fraction of the 1985 Recommended Daily Allowance of 5,000 units.

Unless a pregnant woman made up the shortfall in the remaining meals or ate one liver meal during the week, she would be deficient according to these standards.

As excess vitamin A is stored in the body, one large meal of liver should supply the minimum requirements of vitamin A for a week, but we must bear in mind that some people have difficulty extracting fat-soluble vitamins from their food, plus there is the likelihood of high pesticide levels in the liver meal.

If I were young, pregnant and asthmatic, I would aim for the middle ground and follow Lady Cilento's advice by ensuring my diet contained sufficient vitamin A foods. I would also add 10,000 units of vitamin A, plus about 25O mg of vitamin E.

As previously mentioned, those occasional vitamin A capsules (5,000 units) during my pregnancy certainly did not harm the twins. As babies they possessed an extremely high resistance to infection and this resistance continued throughout kindergarten, school and even continues today, at university.

HOW SAFE ARE OUR ASTHMA DRUGS?

Alarm has been raised in New Zealand over the asthma drug, fenoterol (Berotec®). New Zealand, like Australia, experienced dramatic increases in asthma deaths after 1965 and fenoterol was linked with this increased death rate. A spokesman for the Wellington School of Medicine said:

> 'While modern methods for treating asthma have improved the quality of life of many asthmatics, mortality has continually increased during the period of their introduction and use.'

In May, 1989, the New Zealand Health Department advised doctors treating severe asthmatics, to use alternatives to fenoterol.

To my knowledge, fenoterol is not widely used in Australia. Salbutamol (Ventolin®), however, a similar (but weaker) drug is freely used here and is also suspect.

Why Ventolin® has earned disrepute has not been fully explained. Suddenly we are being told the largest selling asthma drug in Australia could be dangerous with long-term use. Why are we not being told the full story on Ventolin®? Surely simply stating 'it could be dangerous' is not enough?

If Ventolin® puffers are hazardous, what does this make Ventolin® delivered by nebuliser? The dose received by this method is medically estimated to be fifty times that of the puffer. Fifty times!

At an asthma seminar in 1984 attended by world leaders in asthma research, one doctor claimed:

'What I am convinced about, as has been shown in the majority of studies of patients with asthma, is that <u>conventional</u> doses of beta-adrenoceptor agonists do <u>not</u> cause development of tolerance or resistance. I think it is important to state that this applies to conventional doses, <u>but may not be true for nebulised</u>

<u>doses</u>. We are studying long term use in nebulisers, where there is a <u>suggestion that there is development of resistance.</u>'

A further claim by a second doctor is as follows:

'My feeling is that asthmatics are in an unusual position, in that they are given these inhalers to use according to subjective symptoms that they experience; when they do not have relief they get scared and take more of the drug, so it is all very well to say that, under very controlled conditions, they take this dose regularly at such and such a time and you can set up studies to prove that, but, one can never be sure that that is the way that asthmatics use their medihalers. There is a very <u>real possibility</u> that at least a group of these people <u>over use such medication and induce tachyphylaxis</u>.'

The first doctor responded:

'In Britain, patients tend to under use rather than overuse their inhaler, because there has been concern about overusing inhalers, and the dose that is recommended is quite small, so I think that it must be a very small minority who actually really overuse their inhalers. I think that the problem is with <u>nebulisers where the dose is about fifty fold greater</u> and it may be that people are using much larger doses there.'

A third doctor interjected with:

> *The really large doses of beta-adrenoceptor agonists (Berotec®, Ventolin®, Bricanyl® etc.) are given when people come into hospital with bad asthma.'*

As we can see, doubts regarding bronchodilators (Ventolin® etcetera) were being expressed by these experts as far back as 1984.

Further interesting information came from a fourth doctor/researcher, who said:

> *'I remember a case report in the literature on <u>cod-liver oil and asthma,</u> and I think it was referred to in a lecture of Professor Burn some time ago, <u>implying that cod-liver oil was very good in asthmatic diseases</u>. Do you think we have to consider dietary modification of fluidity in membranes as a potentially effective therapy in asthmatic diseases?'*

A fifth added:

> *'That is a difficult question. A couple of years ago, I was on an <u>ad hoc</u> committee of life sciences, to deliberate on how the diet can influence such function. It was concluded that there was no concrete evidence for this type of suggestion.'*

A sixth man finalised the discussion with the comment:

> 'It is interesting that, when you let the discussion run, eventually the nutritional question does emerge and it is obviously an appropriate time for lunch.'

Note: the first doctor said that some asthmatics may overuse their bronchodilating inhalers and induce 'tachyphylaxis.' To most of us, this word sounds positively awesome. But according to the medical dictionary 'tachyphylaxis' means: 'Rapidly decreasing response to a drug or physiologically active agent after a few doses.'

This definition (containing the words <u>rapidly</u> and <u>few</u>) is extremely worrying. Even today asthma sufferers are instructed to use bronchodilators four times daily.

In a letter to the editor of *The Courier Mail* in October 1990, a vice patron of the Asthma Foundation stated that he had received a telex from a drug company which manufactures bronchodilators. This company claimed that two world asthma authorities, who previously warned against long-term use of bronchodilators, have since changed their commentary to read as follows:

'There is no doubt about the safety of asthma relieving drugs such as Ventolin®,

Bricanyl®, Berotec® and Raspolin® — all bronchodilators.'

The vice patron expressed amazement that this turn-about should occur, considering that Berotec® (fenoterol) had been incriminated in the increased mortality rate in New Zealand.

It would seem likely that should there be any concerns about drug tolerance, or overdose reactions from bronchodilators, Queensland would have to experience more problems than say, England. It seems every second asthmatic in Queensland owns or rents a nebuliser. I heard a young mother at an asthma lecture say, 'The kindergarten my child attends has refused to continue attaching children to their nebulisers during the lunch hour, because those without asthma are being neglected.'

Nebuliser sales must be booming in Queensland.

An elderly pensioner rang a Brisbane Open Line radio station to say he required seven or eight asthma prescriptions per week. Another woman rang to say a friend of hers had three children on full-time asthma medication.

An extract from a letter to the magazine *Breathing Space*, January 1987, outlines the regime maintained by a young woman:

2 x 250 SR Nuelin® 3 times a day

Ventolin® 3 x day - 2 puffs

Becloforte® 3 x day - 2 puffs

Nebuliser 3 x day

Bricanyl® 7.5 mg - 1 at night.

Six Nuelin® a day seems incredible to one who gets the jitters from only one tablet. The whole thing is mind boggling. In my opinion there's no wonder this person is ill! The nonchalance with which some asthma sufferers use inhaled bronchodilators seems to indicate that these medications are often regarded as harmless. A secondary school teacher told me he knew of instances where students handed puffers around the entire class. He said they got a 'high' from the puffers.

I wonder if people who abuse bronchodilators connect their headaches, irritability, rapid heart rate and skeletal muscle tremor, with the over-use of their puffer? MIMS (Intercontinental Medical Statistics) states that nebulisers can cause potentially serious disturbance of heart rhythm plus possible heart muscle damage with high doses over long periods.

These are not minor dangers.

The cost to Australia in supplying medication for such a large number of asthma sufferers is astronomical. Former Health Minister, Mr Howe, said on 12th October, 1990, that the Government outlay for asthma amounts to an astronomical fifty million dollars a year. He added, 'Asthma is the most prevalent chronic health problem in Australia.' One wonders how long a government can continue to subsidise these huge amounts. More to the point, I wonder for what period can the body continue absorbing such high levels of drugs before damage or death occurs.

Australians do not appear to share the British fear of inhalers. Actually Australia and New Zealand has a much higher death rate from asthma than England. In 1981 England had a mortality rate (ages 5 - 34 years) of almost 1 per 100,000 of population. (From 'Asthma — Its Management In General Practice'). Australia with 538 deaths in 1981, had approximately 3 per 100,000. In 1987 with 803 deaths, this Australian mortality rate had risen to approximately 5 per 100,000. This is shocking, particularly when countries such as Scandinavia and America, like Britain, have low mortality rates.

Another puzzling aspect of the disease, is that England has had an increase in the overall numbers of asthmatics, whereas Denmark and Finland have not. What are the inhabitants of Denmark and Finland doing right?

Thankfully, results of research published in *The Lancet* of December 1990 indicate a change in the use of bronchodilators is being considered:

> *'A New Zealand study of 88 asthma patients found that only 30% improved when treated with regular doses of the inhaled bronchodilator, fenoterol. Seventy percent improved when treated with the drug only at the time of an asthma attack.*

The Lancet published an accompanying editorial criticising bronchodilators, and called on doctors and drug companies to re-define the use of such drugs in treatment.

> *'Physicians who manage patients with asthma are therefore confronted with the uncomfortable possibility that a mainstay of treatment may be harmful, just when long acting (bronchodilators) are about to be introduced. Enthusiasm for such effective drugs will need to be tempered by the findings of the two new studies.'*

As mentioned earlier in Chapter 10, many people are also concerned about the use of oral steroids in asthma. On a visit to our State Library, I studied an edition of MIMS and found a list of side effects from the oral steroids used in the treatment of asthma. It was frightening.

I wondered whether those on oral steroids would connect symptoms such as insomnia and severe depression (sometimes bordering on psychotic) to these drugs.

I think the oral steroid side effects of cataracts and osteoporosis are commonly known, but what of others cited in MIMS, such as menstrual irregularities, moon face, personality changes, hypertension, peptic ulcer, low resistance to infection, congestive heart failure in susceptible patients and muscle weakness etcetera.

If you are taking steroids, are you aware of these <u>side-effects</u>?

You might say, 'But the effects of vitamin A <u>overdose</u> are also dangerous.' Of course they are — but we must remember that the adverse effects presented in MIMS refers to <u>normal</u> and long-term use of <u>prescribed</u> doses. Overdose is not mentioned.

As we all know, medication is life-saving on occasions, and it <u>must</u> be on hand at all times should an emergency occur.

What is particularly worrying many asthmatics, however, is the sheer quantity of medication they are told to administer. Surely our principal aim must be to reduce the quantity of drugs while still maintaining a good quality of life.

LUKE'S MAGIC PILLS

In June, 1994, Jim told me of a new staff member at his workplace. Margaret was experiencing considerable stress because of the severe asthma of her nine-year-old son, Luke, who had been hospitalised two or three times a year since the age of eighteen months. He was in hospital once again.

Upon his release he was given cortisone tablets and the doctor informed Margaret he would probably develop a moon face as a side effect. Margaret was worried and voiced her concerns to Jim.

Naturally Jim told her about my experience, and Margaret rang me at home. I explained my belief that asthma was a vitamin A deficiency and suggested she try cod or halibut-liver oil capsules (5,000 units of vitamin A) plus 100 mg. vitamin E.

Margaret rang back later to say, 'I told the doctor I was thinking of giving Luke vitamin A for his asthma, and the doctor replied, "Margaret, if vitamin A worked for asthma, everyone would be taking it".'

She added that she had attempted to buy some cod-liver oil capsules from her chemist but he had none. He had no straight vitamin A either and lectured her on its dangers. Vitamin E in 100 mg. doses was also unavailable.

I gave her a vitamin catalogue and from it she ordered the appropriate capsules.

About a week later Jim asked Margaret how Luke was feeling and was told, 'He's back in hospital.'

Margaret rang me after Luke arrived home to say she was thinking of giving Luke two cod-liver oil capsules instead of one. I estimated '10,000 units would be the equivalent of a 25 gram meal of sheep liver, so I felt safe in saying, 'Try it for a few days and see how he goes.'

The following week she rang back. 'Luke has improved out of sight. As soon as he commenced the double dose, his asthma disappeared. Every morning before school he says, "Can I have some of those magic pills?".'

Some months later a thrilled Margaret rang to say that Luke wanted to thank me. He still had no asthma symptoms. Luke's teacher had told her that on "Show and Tell" day, Luke stood bravely in front of the class and said, 'I used to have asthma, but now I don't any more and it's all because of Mrs. Slee's pills.'

The teacher called Luke aside afterwards and asked, 'What's in these pills of Mrs Slee's?'

Luke replied, 'Cod liver oil.'

The teacher was interested, hoping to help a nun at the convent who suffered with asthma.

Luke was the talk of St. Elizabeth's. Many people knew he had always been a severe asthmatic, often missing school because of it, yet here he was — healthy, and at class in spite of the worst smoke and dust haze known in this city.

He attended Cub meetings in the evenings, participated in outside sports activities and didn't require his puffer.

Recently, following a persistent cough, Luke's father was also diagnosed with asthma. He asked Margaret if he could borrow Luke's puffer.

'No way,' she said. 'Take some of his magic pills. If they work for him, they might work for you.'

He was sceptical but he did as he was told, and his cough disappeared. Now he, too, believes in the "magic pills".

In December, 1994, I decided I had to meet this exceptional boy, Luke. When I rang Margaret, she said, 'Luke's been on halibut-liver oil capsules lately, but we've run out of them. Will he be all right for about three days while I order some more?'

'I'm sure he will,' I replied.

However, four days later when I arrived at their home, Margaret said Luke needed his puffer that morning; the first time in six months.

Luke is the couple's only child and obviously much loved. He has dark brown hair, blue eyes and a heart-melting smile, so loving him would be easy.

'I don't think people understand what a serious disease asthma is,' said Luke's father, 'I mean every second person these days seems to have it, but unless you live with it, you just don't know what it's like.'

He outlined the history of Luke's problems which began when he was eighteen months old. 'He coughed every day and night for weeks. I came home one afternoon and he was still coughing. Margaret was on the verge of collapse. Something in me snapped. I picked up the eighteen bottles of antibiotics, made a list of the brand names and cost of each bottle, grabbed Luke and went straight to the hospital.

'I told them we couldn't take any more as Luke hadn't improved at all on the eighteen different antibiotics. I told the doctor we were a one-income family and couldn't afford such expense (approx. $250). We finally received some response. Luke's chest was X-Rayed and the diagnosis came back - 'asthma'. The hospital lent us a large old-fashioned nebuliser and gave us instructions on how to use it. We were totally bewildered by the procedure and in a state of shock from the diagnosis. We went home and attached our screaming eighteen-month-old child to the nebuliser. There was no asthma on either side of the family, but the diagnosis was proven correct that night. We lay waiting for the usual coughing fit. Nothing happened.

'Luke was hospitalised at least twice a year, and he was given his first steroid tablets at three and a half years of age.'

I asked Luke how he'd felt about having to go to hospital. 'I hated it,' he said. 'They put me in a tent full of hot air. I just wanted to escape out of that tent.'

His mother added, 'When Luke was about five he was given twenty children's cortisone tablets per day. He was hospitalised initially for two weeks and kept home from school for an extra three. There was no time for school, delivering the medication took nearly all day.'

I couldn't believe what I was hearing, but I knew it was true.

'By the time he finally went back to school,' said the father, 'he had developed a moon face which caused him much embarrassment. He had to use a large spacer with his puffer and was also teased because of this.'

In desperation, Luke's parents consulted a naturopath whose treatments cost them $350. Luke hated the vile tasting mixtures and although Margaret endured the recommended diet with him, the regime had no effect whatsoever on Luke's asthma.

'This is the first time anything has actually worked.' said Luke's father.

Margaret added, 'Last winter was his best winter ever.'

Luke certainly looks the picture of health. I asked if his colour had always been so good.

'Not at all,' said Carl, 'his lips used to get a

definite blue tinge when he was sick.'

'Did you ever fear you might lose him?' I inquired.

'Yes, once I did. It was when he was about three. The doctor and nurses were working on him, Margaret was holding his hand and I was pacing up and down saying to myself, 'This is it... This is it.'

Margaret said, 'While I was holding Luke's hand, a nursing sister came up to me and said, "For goodness sake, stop molly-coddling him!".'

I could understand the mental torment this couple must have endured.

Recently, after a doctor had examined Luke, Margaret was told that his chest was clear.

'I'm sure that's because of the vitamins he's been taking,' said Margaret.

'It wouldn't be the vitamins,' retorted the doctor. 'It's just the seven-year cycle.' Luke was nine.

Margaret assured me that they didn't wish to "doctor-bash" because they were grateful to Luke's specialist who was a dedicated man. At 1a.m. during freezing weather, he would arrive at the hospital to attend to their son.

They were full of admiration for his strong nerve which enabled him to remain calm while treating extremely ill children some of whom he rescued from death's door.

When the School Nurse came to St Elizabeth's, she rang Margaret at Jim's office to say how thrilled she was at the improvement in Luke's lungs.

Thankfully Luke has now experienced eleven asthma-free months. He now lives a normal life, and hopefully those asthma attacks which caused him such fear and suffering, will eventually fade from his mind.

The sky's the limit now, Luke.

IT HAS FINALLY HAPPENED

I can't believe it! They've gone ahead and done it.

I received a notice from my vitamin distributor informing me that a government regulation passed in July 1993, now forbids over-the-counter sale of any vitamin A exceeding 5,000 units. This vitamin company has ceased manufacturing 10,000 unit capsules. Phone calls to various other retailers brought the same response. I was told, however, that a Sydney company was still producing 9,000 unit tablets. I rang their pharmacist who informed me he was only permitted to sell to doctors, chemists, dentists and hospitals. 'If you want these capsules, you will need a doctor's prescription. It's absolutely ridiculous!' he said. 'This regulation should never have gone through. Our company fought it all on our own. Did you know that 10,000 unit capsules are now registered S4 on the Poisons Register?'

'They can't be!' I exclaimed. 'Only the other day I read that cortisone is marked POISON S4. How can vitamin A be the same?'

'You've got me. Are they going to make people get doctor's prescriptions now to go to the butcher, because 100gm. of liver contains 50,000 units of vitamin A?'

'I know — Is Australia the only country doing this?

'Yes,' he replied, 'you can still buy them everywhere else.'

Following this conversation, I began to wonder, 'Who makes the decision that vitamin A and cortisone should both be classed Poison S4?'

I rang more pharmacists then only to be told that even if I did have a doctor's prescription they would be unable to supply me with 10,000 unit capsules. They had none in stock. They could however, order some for me.

One chemist knew of two companies still selling 10,000 unit capsules. Unfortunately, the first brand, the one belonging to the chemist I spoke to in Sydney, contained fillers which upset my stomach, so that left only one company. Their capsules are based on soy-bean oil which I tolerate well and their headquarters are also in Sydney, so I rang their chemist who advised me: 'Stockpile while you can. We are ceasing the production of 10,000 unit capsules and at the end of the year we commence making only 2,500 unit doses. The authorities say we don't need any extra fat-soluble vitamins.'

'Well, what are people like me supposed to do?' I inquired, 'or aren't there many on the higher doses?'

'Actually,' he said, 'I've had quite a few calls like yours. One lady from Melbourne was absolutely frantic.'

'I can understand why. I'm beginning to think people like me can't absorb fat soluble vitamins from our food.'

'That's right,' he said, 'you probably lack the proper enzymes.'

'I suppose I'll have to send overseas when my stock-pile runs out then?'

'Yes.' he replied.

After some heavy ringing around, I

managed to find three Australia-wide companies still selling 5,000 unit capsules. Unfortunately, one of the brands (the one most easily available) causes me severe abdominal distress. Still the other two types are agreeable. Asthmatics, therefore, requiring only moderate Vitamin A doses, should encounter few difficulties. If, however, the only available dose is 2,500 units, those over forty who need higher doses could be forced to take at least 16 capsules per day and perhaps 24 during mid-winter. This age group would have trouble swallowing not only the capsules but also the cost attached to this bureaucratic overkill.

One chemist was sympathetic to my plight and gave me some helpful advice. 'Eventually you will have to give up trying to find 10,000 unit capsules,' he said, 'so I suggest when that happens, you should try marine lipid concentrate capsules which contain a fish-oil called Omega-3.' I hope it works.

America passed a law forbidding the labelling of vitamin A as poisonous. Australia must do likewise. (Registering vitamin A on the Poison's Register and marking it S4, certainly gives the impression that it is poisonous or at least dangerous.)

How can a product be 'safe' in one country and 'poisonous' in another?

Why is Australia so swift to restrict vitamin A when it is so disgracefully slow in following America's lead in banning dangerous pesticides? American experts believe many pesticides are carcinogenic. Vitamin A is considered by authorities such as Dr Michael B. Sporn, of the American National Cancer Institute, to be one of the chief nutrients in the battle against cancer — and it is allowed in America in strengths deemed 'poisonous' in Australia.

Madness!

While in the city recently, I visited a huge chemist shop and, out of curiosity, asked if they had any vitamin A. The shop assistant replied that they didn't stock vitamin A any more. 'It causes birth defects, you know.' (We can't blame the shop assistant for repeating what she'd been told, but it's worrying to think of the people she may have convinced.)

They did stock cod-liver oil capsules (5,000 i.u.vit.A) so I bought some and was staggered to read the following warning: 'Taking more than five-eighths of a capsule during pregnancy may cause birth defects.' (See chapter 19).

This is good old-fashioned cod-liver oil we're talking about. It's been around since Moses! By the way, how does one take five-eighths of a capsule?

Another shock awaited me on reading the labels on two well-known brands of multivitamin capsules. Neither contained any vitamin A (not even betacarotene) and one brand even declared itself to be 'retinol free'.

NOTE: Retinol is the technical name for basic vitamin A.

It is advisable to read the contents listed on the label before buying multivitamins. You may not be getting any vitamin A at all.

As I still hadn't received any information from Canberra on why this new regulation had been passed, I decided to ring and make inquiries.

I had a lengthy conversation with a bureaucratic gentleman who told me the new regulation was not trying to frighten people off vitamin A and he was upset to hear of my experience in the large chemist shop. He said the regulation was brought in to protect the public from over-dosing, which was a concern in one of the states where there had been publicity about vitamin A preventing cancer. I told him I believed that could be true. He ignored my comment and said there was evidence that overdosing on vitamin A caused birth defects, and he would send me this information. As it transpired I waited nearly ten months.

Here we are, with thousands suffering cancer or asthma, plus umpteen people abusing drugs and all the authorities can do, is worry that someone might overdose on vitamin A! Shouldn't they be shouting from the rooftops, 'Hey, everyone, whatever you do, don't become deficient in vitamin A.'

While waiting for the information from Canberra, my daughter, Melissa, suggested that *The Medical Journal of Australia* might contain relevant information.

After searching through past copies of this journal at the State Library, I found and read an article in the December 1992 issue.

It was a lengthy report on the potential for birth defects of vitamin A, and its 'congeners'. Speaking purely as a lay person there appeared to be sufficient proof to incriminate the drugs which are <u>synthetic derivatives</u> of vitamin A and used in the treatment of acne and psoriasis. However, from the evidence presented in this paper, I still cannot understand why <u>natural Vitamin A</u> would be vilified.

Even after tracking back through medical journals to find the original source of this hysteria, I am still amazed that vitamin A should be so severely restricted. The original evidence appears to be pathetic.

It consists of a list of 18 cases of birth abnormalities presented in a copy of the Rosa FW, Wilk AL, Kelsey FO, (1986) Teratogen Update: Vitamin A Congeners 'Teratology 33:255-364 paper.

The eighteen women listed in the case study gave birth to babies with abnormalities. They had been taking natural vitamin A.

Four of the eighteen examples can be disregarded immediately as they were overdosing, (in some cases, grossly) and we have seen earlier that overdosing causes birth defects in rats.

One woman took 500,000 units during the first and second months. How could anyone survive a dose like that, even if it was only for a few days? (You really would have to wonder about this woman.) Another took 50,000 units of vitamin D. That would also be massive overdosing of that vitamin.

We are left with 14 cases on the list. One contains no dosage information at all, so it must be disregarded. Of the remaining thirteen some were taking doses of 18,000+, some 25,000, some 40,000, some 50,000 and even 60,000 units daily, before and throughout their pregnancy.

Why were these pregnant women taking such high doses of vitamin A? Their ages are not mentioned, but surely few would be over 40.

In young women, most respiratory problems would, I'm sure, respond to much lower doses than those mentioned above.

The anomalies pertaining to these thirteen cases are as follows:-

(a) No data is supplied as to why these women were taking such high doses of vitamin A.

(b) Ages are not mentioned.

(c) No dates are recorded.

(d) No doctor or researcher's name is mentioned.

(e) Some don't even mention the country of origin.

They are so lacking in data that an analytical chemist said,

'Evidence like that would never stand up in a court of law.' No control studies have been carried out either, and the medical journal article added: 'At this time no denominators exist for developing control rates.'

I can't get any extra information on these cases because the details are not published in any scientific paper. They are only on this list which according to a spokesman from the State Library could have been a handout at a presentation.

I spoke to a pharmacist about the eighteen birth defect cases. He too must have seen this paper, because he expressed surprise that vitamin A should have been considered responsible for the birth defects when there was no indication whether the mothers had been smoking marijuana or drinking excess alcohol during the pregnancies.

Canberra finally forwarded the promised 'evidence' of birth defects caused by vitamin A. Incredibly, it was exactly the same 'list' which I'd previously found.

So! this is why pregnant women are warned off all sources of vitamin A in excess of 2,500 units.

If people like me don't come out and call this pathetic, who will?

Who cares enough about vitamin A to raise his/her voice?

Who has the right and the obligation to speak out?

Me, that's who!

There is an interesting section in the 1992 Australian Medical Journal article, which refers to cancer. I quote: '... an absence of retinoids (vitamin A) produces a deregulation of cell growth, similar to that seen in carcinogenesis (cancer).'

This quote is fascinating because my old book on vitamin A, published in 1978, said the same thing.

NOTE: The journal article used the word 'absence' not 'deficiency'.

Are the writers saying that cells containing no vitamin A look like cancer cells? Could it be they look like cancer cells, because they are cancer cells?

The Recommended Daily Allowance for vitamin A has also been changed. According to the 1980 American Chart shown earlier, a male adult and a pregnant woman both require a minimum 5,000 units of vitamin A per day. In 1994 the Australian Health department advised 'The recommended adult daily amount of vitamin A <u>from all sources</u> is 2,500 i.u.'

The words 'from all sources' is amazing.

According to these new daily requirements, eating more than two eggs per day and a cheese sandwich, would be overdosing on vitamin A and if pregnant could cause birth defects!

<u>Someone has it wrong</u>. Very soon, only 2,500 unit capsules will be in our shops. When this happens, theoretically, we should not only require a doctor's prescription to purchase liver, we should also need one for carrots or spinach.

More madness!

We can't survive without vitamin A, so why are the powers-that-be trying so hard to scare everyone off it?

I ask, 'Is vitamin A seen as a threat to drug companies?'

Each day new evidence appears on the adverse effects of asthma medication and the benefits of vitamin A for various cancers, then suddenly only very low doses of this vitamin are available. Is this a coincidence?

While speaking with doctors and chemists, I am continually amazed that they are only interested in the dangers of vitamin A overdose. Very few have been impressed by the fact that I've been free of asthma for fourteen years.

Soon there will be no point paying money to wheedle a prescription from a doctor, because higher doses of this vitamin will not be available. Hopefully, the three companies mentioned earlier, will continue producing 5,000 unit capsules. I predict that the new 2,500 unit doses will cost almost as much as the old 10,000 unit capsules.

Cod-liver oil or A+D wouldn't be suitable for people like me who take high dosages - we'd soon overdose on vitamin D. NOTE: Bio Concepts, Kelvin Grove, Queensland states that doses of Vitamin D, in excess of 4,000 units per day, constitute an overdose.

Beta-carotene, of which only one sixth converts to vitamin A, would be useless. My nutritionist said, 'Only straight vitamin A would work for you, Marian.' I'm sure I couldn't stomach lamb's fry every day and diabetics who cannot convert carotene into vitamin A may also have problems.

If I have to choose between those who parrot current scare-tactics and the teachings of esteemed doctors, I will follow Doctors Pauling, Sporn, and Lady Cilento every time.

When it comes to asthma, I've proven Lady Cilento's teachings are true. Whatever would she say if she were alive today?

This regulation is ridiculous. If vitamin A is 'poisonous', why don't we need a doctor's prescription to purchase whisky? Being treated like an idiot infuriates me; 10,000 unit capsules should be freely available and mothers must not be told moderate amounts of vitamin A cause birth defects.

Let the madness cease.

ADVANTAGES OF VITAMINS OVER DRUGS

Listed below are the tremendous advantages obtained from the use of vitamins (as opposed to drugs) as the principal method of controlling asthma. The most significant of these advantages are:

1. Absence of <u>Side Effects</u>: This is the most wonderful advantage of them all. Unlike sufferers on medication, asthmatics who take the correct dose of A, E and if necessary C, would have no symptoms, no side-effects and could enjoy life to the fullest.

2. <u>Eliminates Fear</u>: Although vitamins take about twenty hours to work, they have a tremendous advantage in that they continue working for at least twelve hours and usually much longer. This eliminates the perpetual worry of parents and patients — that puffers might be mislaid when the asthma sufferer is away from home.

3. <u>Vitamins are Easy and Pleasant to Take</u>: No puffers or machines required. No embarrassment in public. Taking vitamins is more socially acceptable than using a puffer.

4. <u>Cost</u>: The outlay for vitamin treatment depends upon a person's age and the severity of their disease. For children the expense is minimal. If purchased from the distributor, they would consume less than $5 worth of vitamins per months in winter, half that in summer. The costing for adults would range from $5 to $20 per month in winter. Much less in summer. Vitamins are cheaper and fresher if bought in bulk from the distributor.

5. <u>Less Concern Over Long-term Effects</u>: Many asthmatics (and parents of asthmatics) worry about the long-term effects of medication — I did. With vitamin treatment, there is little cause for concern. Any detrimental effect from vitamin overdose is quickly reversed by ceasing or reducing the

vitamin. One wonders if adverse reactions to drugs are so easily reversed.

6. <u>Treatment can be Increased Without Fear</u>: During times of severe asthma, vitamin dosages can be significantly increased without fear of over-dose. Lady Cilento said adults can safely take 60,000 to 90,000 units of vitamin A for a period of three months. The safety margin for drugs is dramatically lower than for vitamins.

7. <u>Most Asthma Drugs Merely Suppress Symptoms</u>: With vitamins, there are no symptoms. Remember the mother of the twelve-year-old girl. She said, 'If they invented a drug as good as this, it would be hailed a wonder drug!'

8. <u>Increased Energy Levels</u>: Provided the correct amount of vitamins are taken, there is a substantial increase in natural (not drug induced) energy.

9. <u>Vitamins Work Quickly</u>: AS A PREVENTATIVE, vitamins A and E work faster than inhaled corticosteroids (Becotide® etc.) which can require up to three weeks to take effect. Despite the popular belief that vitamins require months to be effective, most asthmatics have reported improvement <u>within a few days</u>.

10. <u>Vitamins and Drugs are Compatible</u>: Although I have always tried to avoid medication, many people combine the two with success.

FINAL
RECOMMENDATIONS

After reading this book, I'm confident you will feel a new optimism towards your asthma. I'm sure your life-style will be happier and healthier and I hope you will not allow 'scare tactics' to dampen that optimism.

Someone once said 'Fear is Faith in Disaster' and it often seems fear can be stronger than love or life itself. Fear can shrivel us up; reducing our ability to 'have a go' at achieving the good health for which we were designed.

One of the best antidotes to fear is hope. Does anyone, however expert, have the right to tell another, 'There is no hope.' How can they know the future with so much certainty.

Don't allow yourself to be frightened off vitamin A.

Keep in mind, ANYTHING is dangerous in overdose, and symptoms of vitamin A overdose are completely reversible within a few days.

THERE IS NOTHING TO FEAR

Rather than rejecting new ideas, a wise person would agree with my nutritionist who says 'I'm for whatever works.'

I would like to leave you with my personal Winter Health Tips in the hope that you might find them helpful. Bear in mind I live in Brisbane, and despite popular opinion, winter can be extremely cold. Those from warmer areas would have fewer problems coping with sudden temperature drops but colds and influenza know no boundaries.

<u>Marian's Winter Health Tips</u>
1. Be aware of fluctuating temperatures.
2. Take vitamins every day in winter, using the <u>minimum</u> amount required to eliminate symptoms.
3. Wear a spencer or woollen vest during cold weather. (Keep the chest warm.)
4. Invest in an electric blanket.

5. Blow-dry hair immediately after shampooing and take a good dose of vitamin C. This helps prevent colds, influenza and ear problems.
6. Avoid taking hot showers immediately before a night out.
7. Wash hands often in winter, as infections are spread by hand contact.
8. Keep warm. If the body uses all its energy maintaining normal temperature, it has nothing left to fight infection.
9. Asthmatics should suspect mild asthma if feeling persistently tired. I always increase A and maybe E. (Persistent fatigue, however, is not always asthma-related).
10. If increasing A and E doesn't ease definite asthma symptoms, I treat as a viral infection by increasing vitamin C powder to three teaspoons per day for five days. Use much smaller doses for children.
11. Vitamin E must not be increased quickly if you suffer high blood pressure.
12. Do not take iron tablets and vitamin E at the same time as iron can cancel out vitamin E. (from *The Vitamin Conspiracy*).
13. I usually commence vitamins in late February or early March. Temperatures can drop suddenly around this time.

14. If overcome by a cold or influenza, don't assume vitamins have failed and give up. This is the time to increase vitamin intake if asthma is to be avoided.

15. Always include plenty of vitamin A rich foods in your diet and use garlic occasionally in cooking. Garlic has a reputation for being beneficial in asthma — not so for romance!

16. In case of emergencies, make sure asthma medications are on hand and up to date.

17. Asthma should never be taken lightly. Severe asthmatics should organise a crisis plan with a doctor. A Peak Flow Meter is advisable.

No one can know the future. For the rest of our lives, these vitamins may be all that I and others on this program, will require.

If, while rearing a large family, I was continually suffering asthma symptoms or side-effects from drugs, I'd have found life impossible so I was virtually forced to find a cure for my malaise. You can understand then why I am so excited about this vitamin treatment.

I feel sure, that we who have known success with vitamins, will always be grateful for QUALITY OF LIFE, and isn't that the most important thing of all?

BIBLIOGRAPHY
This is not the place for a definitive bibliography on Asthma. The following is simply a list of books which helped me.

Adams, R. and Murray, F. *Improving Your Health With Vitamin A* (U.S.A.: Larchmont Books, 1978).

Antia, F.P. *Clinical Dietetics and Nutrition* (Bombay: Oxford University Press, 1989).

Atkins, R.C. *Dr Atkins' Nutrition Breakthrough* (New York: William Morrow and Co. Inc., 1981).

Bingham, S. *Dictionary of Nutrition* (London: Barrie & Jenkins, 1977).

Cilento, P. Lady *Medical Mother* (Australia: *The Courier Mail* Publication, 1982).

Cilento, P. Lady *Vitamin and Mineral Deficiencies* (Australia: Pitman Publishing Pty. Ltd., 1983).

Colgan, M. *Your Personal Vitamin Profile* (Great Britain: Blond & Briggs, 1984).

Fried, J.J. *The Vitamin Conspiracy* (U.S.A.: Clarke Irwin & Co., 1975).

Gerras, C *The Complete Book of Vitamins* (U.S.A.: Rodale Press, Emmaus, PA, 1977).

Gildroy, A. *Vitamins and Your Health* (Great Britain: Unwin Paperbacks, 1983).

Gregg, I. *Asthma - Its Management in General Practice* (Australia: Update Publications, 1985).

Hayes, W.J.Jr. *Toxicology of Pesticides* (Baltimore: the Williams and Wilkins Company, 1975).

Lankford, T.R. and Steward, P.J. *Foundations of Normal and Therapeutic Nutrition* (New York: Wiley, 1986).

Meillon, R. and Reading, C. *Relatively Speaking* (Sydney: Fontana Australia, 1985).

Morley, J. *Beta-Adrenoceptors in Asthma* (London: Academic, 1984).

Newbold, H.L. *Vitamin C Against Cancer* (U.S.A.: Stein & Day, 1979).

Snyder, W., Kennedy, E., and Aubusson P., *Biology - The Spectrum of Life* (Melbourne: Oxford University Press,1990).

Wills, E.D. *Biochemical Basis of Medicine* (Bristol: Wright, 1985).